SEEING THE INVISIBLE

SEEING THE INVISIBLE

by
Anne Sandberg

Logos International
Plainfield, New Jersey

To my friend, Joanne Michell, whose witness set my feet on
    "The path of the just [which] is as the shining light that
    shineth more and more unto the perfect day." Proverbs
    4.18

And to my daughter, Betty Nelson, whose perceptive
criticisms and suggestions clarified and strengthened the
message of this book.

CONTENTS

SECTION ONE

About Heaven

"God helps us become aware of the brevity of time and the endlessness of eternity. He teaches us a truth that we innately knew, but didn't know how to put into words—that we were made for another world. . . ."

Bill Popejoy in the *Pentecostal Evangel*

CHAPTER 1

Heaven

This book is about heaven—
heaven as described in the scriptures—
heaven as seen in authentic dreams and visions—
heaven as visited by those whose spirits left their bodies.

John the Apostle saw heaven in a vision; St. Paul was transported to paradise; hundreds of contemporary Christians have also seen heaven, some being taken there in spirit. But, for the most part, before one goes to heaven, he must die. And death is an ugly word, particularly to those who have experienced the anguish of standing beside the corpse of a loved one who has just expired. For a Christian, that event becomes tolerable only by the knowledge that from that empty grey shell lying before him, the spirit has taken its flight into a place called heaven.

Paradoxically, honest Christians will sometimes admit to a lack of enthusiasm about this "Beautiful Isle of Somewhere," which they vaguely imagine to be a nebulous place through which float spooky spirits robed in vapor. Others envision the blessed souls lounging upon a grassy sward, blissfully strumming harps or attending a great big, never-ending church service.

This concept of heaven would hardly appeal to the person who begins to look at his watch, should the Sunday morning service run a few minutes past noon. Even some Christians with a deep love for God and delight in His presence, if they were truthful, would confess to uneasiness about what they will do with so much time on their hands.

Besides this uncertainty, a percentage of Christians wonder: "How do we know whether the scriptures about heaven are meant to be taken literally or symbolically? Are there really streets of gold or is gold a type of purity? Those Bible expressions—'city, country, place, world-to-come, river, trees, fruit'—are they symbolic or literal? Surely heaven can't be that real!"

Because these matters often leave a Christian with furrowed brow and a sense of guilt over his secret doubts, he generally pushes thoughts of death and heaven into some unused chamber of his mind, taking them out briefly only after having attended a funeral.

Another device, particularly of the unconverted, is to argue, "Oh well, no one has ever been to heaven and come back to tell us what it is like, so I might as well forget about it until the time comes and concentrate on living."

The fact is, however, that some actually have been in heaven and have returned to tell us about it!

Jesus was there and told us He was going back to prepare a place for us. The Apostle Paul spent some time in paradise. Though he disappointed us by not telling what he saw, he did give us some enticing but generalized facts. When John received his revelation on the isle of Patmos, he was summoned into heaven and shown many scenes there. Moreover, Paul the Apostle assured us that ". . . no mere man has ever seen, heard or even imagined what wonderful things God has ready for those who love the Lord" (1 Cor. 2:9 TLB).

4

In this book we will look at a number of the hundreds of accounts of reliable witnesses who have experienced heaven in different ways. Some of these witnesses were granted visions or dreams, others glimpsed the next world at the moment of passing over. A number were declared clinically dead but returned to life to describe what they saw. A few went into trances as the Apostle Paul did, their spirits being literally transported to heaven.

Although these accounts cover a great range of time—from John Bunyan's visions in about 1650 to the accounts recorded in *Life after Life* by Raymond Moody in 1975—and locations as far apart as Lahore, India to Chicago, Illinois, yet many of the stories are so similar and in some details almost identical, that it would be difficult to question their validity.

Some people, and I have been among them, are rather skeptical about dreams and visions being credible conveyers of God's truth. We want to be sure that these experiences proceed from stable, mature and respected Christians and from personalities who are not considered "visionary" in that sense of the word. Still, to discount this method of God communicating with man would be to deny hundreds of such accounts recorded in the Bible.

Personally, any remaining doubts as to the validity of this means were removed after I read *Supernatural Dreams and Visions*, by Carmen Benson. This book is a thorough study of dreams and visions in the Bible and indicates a surprising number of times in which God communicated with His people in this way.

My further hesitances were also greatly minimized by the recent accounts of doctors and psychologists whose researches were recorded in a positive way by national newspapers.

From my reading of the Bible I am convinced that God

intends these supernatural experiences to be projected beyond the sacred pages, unto the end of time (e.g. Mark 16:17; Acts 2:17).

I have included excerpts from older books, written in the literary style of another era, which had been popularly read and accepted by the Christians of their day. Other books which I researched have been written by well known, more contemporary authors in the early 1900s. But in 1975 and 1976 came the big surprise when national newspapers began publishing the findings of scientists concerning the probability of life after death. These will be detailed later.

I have also included in this book experiences of people with whom I am personally acquainted, whose witness is reliable because I know them to be stable Christians.

Though we certainly do not give the same credence and authority to these experiences that we do to the Bible, yet a comparison will indicate that in most cases, rather than violating they corroborate scripture, but in much more detail than the outlines and suggestions given us there.

In the writing of this book I am motivated by three purposes:

1. To remind ourselves that we will one day die and go to heaven, if we are Christians.

2. To show that heaven is as real a place as earth. And to assure us that those who go there will be doing something vastly more satisfying and creative than strumming a harp forevermore.

By describing in fuller detail the reality and happiness of heaven, I hope that any feelings of dread over the thought of death will be replaced by joyful anticipation. For death is not the end, but for the Christian the beginning of a higher and infinitely superior form of life.

3. The most important reason for writing this book is to show that our rewards, types of service and capacities for

fellowship with God in the "world to come" will be in proportion to the degree of growth and spiritual maturity we have achieved while on earth. The greatest mistake a Christian can make is to arrive in heaven not having attained his fullest potential of spiritual growth.

CHAPTER 2

Is There a Literal Heaven?

All she could remember was that as she lay on the operating table, suddenly she was out of her body—looking down at her own corpse surrounded by doctors and nurses—and hearing a nurse say, "Doctor, her pulse is going."

Then Mrs. Julia Ruopp felt herself going down a long passageway, eventually emerging into an "overwhelmingly wide space of light—a pulsing, living light which cannot be described in words."

In a moment she stood before what looked like an enormous convex window and realized that she was "looking through a window into one bright spot of heaven."

"What I saw there," she continued, "made all earthly joys pale into insignificance. . . . As I sat there drinking in the beauty, gradually I became aware of a Presence: a Presence of joy, harmony and compassion. My heart yearned to become a part of this beauty."

Fifteen minutes after her visit to this part of heaven, Mrs. Ruopp's spirit returned to her body, just as the nurse exclaimed, "She's coming to" ("The Window of Heaven," *Guideposts*, October 1963, pp. 28-31).

9

The October 16, 1975 issue of the *Chicago Tribune* contained an article of startling significance. Dr. Elisabeth Kubler-Ross, author of *On Death and Dying* was formerly with the University of Chicago and is an authority on the psychiatric aspects of death and dying. After attending and counseling thousands of dying patients she concluded, "I know beyond the shadow of a doubt that there is life after death." She based her conviction on interviews with hundreds of men and women who were either dying or who were declared legally dead and revived to tell what they had seen in the intervening period.

On May 23, 1976 the *Chicago Tribune* printed an article (reprinted from the *National Observer*, 1976, © Dow Jones, Inc.) in which similar experiences were recorded, listing a number of doctors whose findings amount to what they almost, but which they could not quite, admit to be "scientific proof."

There is life after death. And there is a heaven in which that life will be lived. Scripture declares it and the experiences of hundreds corroborate this fact.

No writer of any book in the Bible tries to prove the existence of heaven; he simply states it as fact. From Genesis to Revelation references to heaven abound. It is neither a symbolic word nor a figure of speech. It is a definite place, a city which hath foundations. Hardly anyone would dispute that this is what the biblical authors themselves believed. And it is good to know that what they believed has been confirmed by hundreds of people whose faith was temporarily made sight.

Marietta Davis was taken into heaven while she lay in a nine-day coma. Her book, *Scenes Beyond the Grave*, was first published in 1850, and went through twenty-nine editions. In it she tells that as she and her angelic guide rose higher and higher, she perceived "an orb brighter than the sun with pure light radiating from it." As they entered the outer expanse of paradise she saw beauty, heard music and felt happiness beyond anything she could have ever imagined.

During an outpouring of the Holy Spirit in the Adullam Ophanage in China in the early 1900s ragged beggar children had received scripturally accurate visions of heaven. These were recorded by H.A. Baker in two of his books (*Visions Beyond the Veil*, and *Heaven and the Angels*, reprinted by Master Productions, San Diego, California).

Because many of the children involved in these heavenly experiences were very young and most of them completely ignorant of Bible teaching, it helped to confirm to the leaders of the orphanage that they were of supernatural origin. Another confirming factor was that several children received the same vision simultaneously, neither having communicated with the other. Some visions were seen by children as young as six years old, in such a manner that they felt they were present in heaven.

In some cases the children seemed to have been actually transported to heaven, and with the candor of innocence, their faces transformed with rapture, described in minute detail various scenes in heaven. They saw predeceased friends and spoke as though they had visited a tangible, though greatly superior, world.

In his book of visions, Sadhu Sundar Singh, a Christian mystic of India, tells the story of a dying saint. A few minutes before this man died, he saw heaven opened and angels and saints coming for him. When he began to rapturously describe what he saw, someone present whispered "His mind is wandering." The dying man heard the remark and replied, "No, it is not. I am quite conscious. I wish you could see this wonderful sight. I'm sorry it is hidden from your eyes. Goodbye, we will meet again in the next world." And he closed his eyes and died (*Visions of Sadhu Sundar Singh* [Minneapolis: Osterhus, n.d.], p. 25).

When General Bramwell Booth of the Salvation Army became seriously ill, lost consciousness and went to heaven, he later said that his next sensation was beyond description (*Visions* [London: Salvation Army, 1906], p. 9). Mrs. Elizabeth Bossert of Fenwich, Canada, died in 1948 and went to heaven for one hour, then returned saying she had seen the gates of heaven open and a dazzling spirit standing beside it (*My Visit to Heaven* [Jacksonville, Florida: Higly, 1968], p. 11). Recently she wrote me that when she again became desperately ill in July, 1975, for three days she had glimpses of "the saints being welcomed home. No words can tell of the grandeur of that welcome celebration. My brother died during this time and I saw him enter heaven. The angels were floating in the air . . . bells were chiming . . ."

(Incidentally, though I have had very few other-world experiences, I did literally hear these same chimes just before my husband died. I was aware they had something to do with announcing his arrival.)

The *Pentecostal Evangel* (July 8, 1973) related what happened to Mrs. Clara Hinkel when she was dead for a few moments. "It seemed to the dying woman that she floated upward apart from her body and was able to look down into the room where she saw her own still form. . . . In the spirit she drifted to a beautiful place."Jesus was there and spoke to her, but told her she had to return to earth for a while.

In *Visions of Heaven and Hell* Robert Young says that Miss D. was taken to heaven and described it as infinitely exceeding in beauty and splendor anything she had ever seen. When she came out of her trance, she announced that Mr. B. had just died, for she saw him enter heaven. Since she had been bedfast, she had no way of knowing this; but later investigation revealed that he had just died at the moment

Miss D. had seen him enter heaven (Dallas: Voice of Healing, n.d., p. 37).

Judson B. Palmer in his pamphlet *The Child of God Between Death and Resurrection* (Minneapolis: Osterhus, 1967 [17th ed. reprint], p. 27) records the experience of a dying Christian woman. During her semiconscious state she looked intently into the far distance and said she saw a child named Mamie, also a man they had called Grandpa enter heaven. Her attending physician was so impressed that he later looked into this and was astonished to learn that each of them had died at the exact time his patient had seen them.

In *Life after Death,* a small booklet containing reprints from *Guideposts* magazine, Dr. Norman Vincent Peale said "Time and again it has been reported of people on the brink of death that they seem to become aware of a great radiance or hear beautiful music or see the faces of departed loved ones who are apparently waiting for them across the line. Are these just hallucinations? I don't think so. Several of them have happened within my own family" (Carmel, N.Y.: Guideposts Associates, 1963, p. 3).

During the encephalitis epidemic in August, 1975, a twenty-three-year-old Christian, Donna Foresgren of Oak Lawn, Illinois, became fatally ill. One morning she said to her roommate in the hospital, "I had a most wonderful dream of a beautiful place. I am going there and I am going to begin a whole new life." Shortly after this, in a clear, strong voice and her mind perfectly rational, she phoned her mother saying, "Mom, I am going to die." She died the following Sunday, face glowing and radiant.

With such an array of incidents (and a great many more not recorded here), it would seem easier to believe than not to. For many years I had heard of dying people talking about what they saw and had always believed that they were delirious. But after three years of research, I have read and heard of so many similar incidents that I am now convinced that they actually saw into heaven.

What so many witnesses saw, hundreds of whose testimonies are not recorded, would seem to constitute a strong evidence that the heaven mentioned in the Bible as "the world to come" is a literal and very real place.

CHAPTER 3

Location

One warm spring night, some months after my husband died, I looked up into the starry sky. My gaze followed the veil-like band of stars called the Milky Way, into which is embedded our own solar system.

"He is in heaven, way up there," I mused, "somewhere far beyond what I can see and millions of light years beyond the probings of our most powerful telescopes." I wondered in just what specific part of that wide dome, arching above the earth, heaven is located.

In the Greek New Testament there are three words that refer to heaven. Interestingly, when we examine them together, they speak of a three-tiered universe. They are *ouranos*, *mesouranema*, and *epouranios*. The latter two words are formed, basically, by adding prefixes to the basic word for heaven, *ouranos*, which is used most widely and generally by the New Testament writers. But, in relation to the other two words, we may take it to refer to the immediate atmosphere of our planet (Matt. 24:35). Above it is the middle heaven, *mesouranema*, which refers to the whole planetary system of galaxies that comprise the universe. It is, humanly speaking, the highest heaven in that

15

it represents the full extent of time and space (Rev. 14:6). But above and beyond *mesouranema* is *epouranios* (Eph. 1:3). This is the peculiar domain of God whose throne, Paul said, is "far above all heavens" (Eph. 4:10). It is inadequate to speak of this realm as if it were in spatial relationship to *ouranos* and *mesouranema,* since it is apart from time and space, but there is no other way to speak which our minds can grasp, so we must speak in spatial terms, like it or not. And thus we ask, where is this *epouranios?*

Many scriptures refer to heaven as being "up," but where is up, when you consider that the world is round?

As the world rotates on its axis, one point is always the same and that is up, which is north. The compass always points toward the north star. The geographic and magnetic poles of the earth are always kept pointing north.

A number of scriptures suggest that heaven may be located in the north. Ps. 48:2—"Beautiful for situation, the joy of the whole earth, is mount Zion *on the sides of the north,* the city of the great King" (italics mine). Isa. 14:13-14—Lucifer boasted . . ." I will sit also upon the mount of the congregation in the sides of the north; . . . I will be like the most High." Lev. 1:11—The burnt offering was to be killed on the side of the altar northward before the Lord. Ezek. 1:4-28—In the vision of Ezekiel, the glory of God in the whirlwind always came from the north. Ps. 75:6—Implies that promotion comes from the north.

When Elizabeth Bossert was taken to heaven, she said "Suddenly I began to hear strains of sweet heavenly music. . . . As I lay there and heard it floating in *from the north,* my soul began to get blessed. . . . Things of earth faded. . . . It was not long until I saw a large body of light *in the north"* (*My Visit,* p. 7, italics mine).

Since scripture and visions seem to place the location of heaven in this way, could heaven be situated in the general

16

area of the North Star?

There is no longer any mystery concerning the first atmospheric heaven; even grade school children know that it is a blanket of air which completely surrounds our earth, keeping us warm by night and insulating us by day from the sun's powerful rays.

Of the second—the starry heavens—astronomers have filled volumes containing such precise information as the diameter of our solar system, the speed at which our earth spins (some 67,000 miles per hour), the distance of stars in the most remote galaxy, speed of travel, chemical composition—though they are millions of light years away!

But no astronomer knows how far beyond the most distant star ever photographed that the place called heaven is located, or whether some of the farthermost galaxies—so distant that they appear as minute points of light—may constitute a part of heaven.

Several of those who were taken into heaven saw part of our solar system as they passed through the first and second heaven on their way to the city of God.

Marietta Davis is the young woman who had been in a coma for nine days, during which time her spirit was taken to heaven. While being conducted to heaven, her guide said to her, "Behold the countless planetary hosts . . . suns and systems of suns moving in silence and harmony. The vast expanse is occupied . . . with universes constituted in infinite wisdom" (*Scenes*, p. 21).

John Bunyan, writing about three hundred years ago, also described his experience when in vision he was taken into heaven: "By this time we were got above the sun, whose vast and glorious body, so much greater than the earth, moved round the great expanse wherein it was placed. . . .

"My conductor told me this mighty, immense hanging globe of fire was one of the great works of God. It always

17

keeps its constant course and never has the least irregularity in its diurnal or its annual motion; and so exceeding glorious is its body that had not my eyes been greatly strengthened, I could not have beheld it.

"Nor were those mighty globes of fire we call the fixed stars less wonderful; whose vast and extreme height, so many leagues above the sun, makes them appear like candles in our sight. And yet they hang within their spheres without support in a pure sea of ether. Nothing but His word that created them could keep them in their station.

"These are all but the scaffolds and outworks to that glorious building wherein the blessed above inhabit that house not made with hands, eternal in the heavens . . ." (*Visions of Heaven and Hell* [Swengal, Pennsylvania: Reiner, n.d.] pp. 13-14).

John Bunyan and Marietta Davis were permitted very small glimpses of our star family which consists of the sun, nine planets, satellites, hundreds of asteroids and comets, billions of meteoric particles. This solar system is set into the Milky Way—that band of stars which seems to divide our sky.

Its hazy, cloud-like appearance is because the Milky Way is composed of one hundred billion stars thickly packed in the center and thinner on its two spiral arms and is so far away that the individual stars are blurred together to the naked eye.

Our own solar system is tremendously large, but one astronomer has figured that there are about ten million other planetary systems beside our own, all within the Milky Way.

As if these amazing facts were not enough, the Psalmist says of these millions of galaxies of innumerable billions of stars that "He [God] determines and counts the number of the stars; He calls them all by their names" (147:4, TAB).

Location

Does life exist on any planet beside our own? The Bible does not tell us, but astronomers are now suggesting this possibility. It could be, they say, that even within our own galaxy, which consists of about ten million planetary systems similar to our own, that there might be planets capable of sustaining life.

This is speculation of course. But we do know that "up," perhaps in the northern part of that immensity of space, is the area which Jesus called "My Father's house," and in which are "many mansions" (John 14:1).

The heaven and the heaven of heavens cannot contain God (1 Kings 8:27). And when we consider the vastness of this ever-expanding universe in which new galaxies are still being formed, one wonders whether heaven could possibly be confined to one comparatively limited local planet or area.

From an article in the *Pentecostal Evangel* entitled "The Ultimate Destiny of the Church," (© 1969 by The General Council of the Assemblies of God, used by permission) written by Frank Boyd we quote several provocative excerpts which he says may "stimulate some questions and attempt an answer."

He who created man and placed him in a material universe that is infinite in its scope will not confine him to a limited existence for all eternity. True, we are given glimpses in the Book of Revelation chapters 21 and 22, of the heavenly city, the abode of the saints, with its beauties, its appointments, its extent, its delights. But we must remember that the heavenly city is but the place of "the throne of God and of the Lamb" (Rev. 22:3) the place from which is exercised His sovereignty over the universe.

Astronomers have come to the conclusion that space is infinite and that the heavenly bodies, as

19

the Scripture says, cannot be numbered. . . .

Are these numberless worlds only lights in the firmament to illuminate our little earth at night? Do we have any ultimate relation to them? Are any of them inhabited? We do not know the answer to the latter question, but we believe they will be needed and prepared for habitation in God's eternal future, in the development and expansion of a redeemed humanity.

Revelation 22:3 tells us that "His [God's] servants shall serve Him" and that service is to be administrative and regal as Revelation 22:5 clearly states—"they shall reign forever and ever." Over what shall the saints reign? Over the heavenly city? That city will surely be our abode, the habitation of the Bride of the Lamb; but may it not be that the heavenly city will be the headquarters from which God and His servants shall rule over an infinite, ever-expanding universe?

We shall first reign with Christ during the Millenium over the earth . . . but beyond that millennial kingdom lie "new heavens and a new earth, wherein dwelleth righteousness" (2 Pet. 3:13). The gates of the heavenly city which are never closed surely must open toward something. Will it not be upon the infinitely wide expanses of the heavenly realms of wondrous beauties, upon whose myriads of worlds which fill infinite space and which we will have the ability and privilege to visit? In other words, "the starry universe is the Christian's future empire," as Dr. Horace C. Stanton put it. . . . What would have happened had our first parents in Eden not failed in the test but had gone on in perfect obedience, morally and otherwise, multiplying as God told them to? They would have filled this earth; and then what? Many of them probably would have had to be transported to other worlds to begin a new life there. . . .

Dr. Horace C. Stanton . . . says "God is everywhere; and He is everywhere all the time. . . . But, if He dwells throughout the entire universe and dwells there all the time, then the entire universe must be His house. . . . This is the Father's home. And if the Prince Royal was slain to bring us into it, will the Father keep us in a single apartment of that house forever? Not even allow us to see this abode the Prince has built? Christ says 'In my Father's house are many mansions [abiding places]. I go to prepare a place for you.' But God's house is greater than His footstool, greater than His throne. . . . God's house is the universe."

Hence, these mansions He is preparing for us are not part of His footstool or part of His throne. They extend far away, beyond both footstool and throne—beyond earth and any local heaven. Why then must they not be the starry world, if not the starry world themselves?

Can they be anywhere else, if indeed anything else? Our abodes will not be confined to a local heaven alone. They will sweep beyond this, through the heaven of heavens. However numerous may be the dustlike clouds of stars, we are the Creator's children; and these crowded nebulae, packed with orbs as thick as the ocean beach with sands, are the many mansions of the house fitted up for His abode and ours.

A number of contemporary religious writers share the same views expressed above. But since the scripture is silent, we can only imagine with awe when we contemplate the planetary heavens, that our heavenly Father and His Son and His Spirit created and inhabit eternity.

This, then, is the Christian's future hope and home—a place in the Father's house to which he will go after his spirit leaves his body. Whether that place be located in the north, or whether the "many mansions" mean more than one unit in the immense planetary system, really does not matter. What is important is that where He is, there will we be also.

CHAPTER 4

What Happens Immediately after Death?

Scripture tells us that upon death a Christian is absent from the body and present with the Lord (2 Cor. 5:6-8). But that does not necessarily mean *immediately* present with the Lord. Among the many cases which have come to my attention—several of which have been mentioned in daily newspapers—in the interval between death and entrance into the next world, various things have happened.

When Julia Ruopp died, she felt her spirit leave her body, then found herself looking down upon her own corpse, which was surrounded by doctors and nurses (*The Window of Heaven*, P. 29).

This has been a frequent experience of those who died and were revived.

Dr. Kubler-Ross, in the October 16, 1975, *Chicago Tribune* article said "Most of the patients said they were floating a few feet above their bodies, watching the resuscitation efforts. They could accurately describe the scene, the details of what was said and the comings and goings of the rescuers and observers."

Recently these cases have begun to move out of the realm of "absolutely not" to "perhaps," and into the view found in the headlines of a second *Tribune* article: "Life after Death, science utters a sheepish 'I believe.' "

A few scientists and perhaps many more who are "secret believers" no longer insist that these experiences are hallucinations.

Dr. Charles Garfield who has worked for many years with cancer patients at the Cancer Research Institute of the University of California in San Francisco says in this article "Who knows? . . . We were forced to the conclusion that the earth is not the center of the universe. We've been forced to accept things that seemed more ridiculous than this" (*Chicago Tribune*, May, 1976).

The article in the *Tribune* on this subject published on the front page of the May 23, 1976 issue (reprinted from *The National Observer*) discusses views of Dr. Raymond Moody, who has written *Life after Life*. Dr. Moody, a former philosophy professor with a second degree in medicine, who interviewed hundreds, says of his book that this collection of incidents of out-of-body experiences did not necessarily indicate proof. Still, the reading of such incidents as are there recorded brought him, as well as an increasing number of scientific minds, to the conclusion that they are no longer sure that there is no communication with the other side.

Dr. Moody tells of an elderly woman having a heart attack, who felt herself drift to the ceiling. As she looked down, she heard one nurse say, "Oh my God, she's gone." As the spirit of the elderly woman watched the various attempts at resuscitation, she wondered why they were so excited because she said, "I'm just fine now." This is typical of other cases researched.

If we now ask why we have not previously heard of such happenings, we would answer that they have been quite common, but heretofore those who had these experiences kept the matter secret for fear they would be considered unstable mentally.

This was the case with a woman who attends our prayer meeting. When she heard that I was writing this book, she told me something astounding. She said that one day after a funeral, she tried to comfort friends by relating her out-of-the-body experience, but was ridiculed. She then determined to keep it secret, telling it only to a clergyman and one other person. I was now the third. She gave me permission to tell her story, but wishes to remain anonymous.

As she told me with utmost candor and simplicity what had happened to her, I was amazed at how it coincided in many details with experiences I had already read about. In a letter to me, with her permission to use it, she wrote her story:

"I do believe in life after death because of my experience. Lying in the hospital bed with excruciating pain, I knew if I moved only slightly, I'd never make it.

"There were two doctors and two nurses watching and whispering something about me. Finally they left. Moments later I heard a voice that came from within me saying, 'I do not have to put up with that' [meaning the pain].

"After that I found myself standing and feeling extremely well; no pain. (At that time I thought they gave me very good medication that healed me so quickly.)

"The light in the room became brighter and seemed to glow. There was love in the air (no fear). My eyesight and hearing improved 100%. My mind was very alert. I remembered everything. My personality and character were the same. (At this point I did not know that I was out of my body.)

"Then I felt myself float up, I was light, weightless. When I looked up I noticed and said, 'How can it be? I never did that before. I'm only two inches away from the ceiling and about twelve inches away from the wall.' This was a shock and quickly I looked at myself standing there. I had two feet, legs, hands, a neck and head. I'm alive. Very happy. Also noticed I had a new dress on, at least I did not remember buying it or having it. It was a white dress, the white seemed to glow and it had tiny pink and blue rosettes scattered about six to eight inches apart. The dress was beautiful. I was young, about twenty years old and slim. I loved what I saw, so why should I be concerned if I'm close to a ceiling?

"Then I decided to look around the room. On the first bed from the door there was an ugly body. It looked like a corpse. I did not like it. Quickly I turned away and as I did this, I caught a glimpse of the robe and gown that body had. I could not understand, why she's wearing my robe and gown. To me it was strange and I did not like it.

"I decided to see who it was. That body was lying on the right side and with extremely good eyesight I saw every line and wrinkle of that face, also her hairdo. With surprise, I screamed, 'It is I!' (How can it be me? The skin color was like a corpse and it didn't move or breathe.)

"Something happened. I knew then that I was out of the body. Shocked at first, but I preferred my living body (soul) and definitely did not like that thing on the bed. I really decided I did not care, because I was alive and feeling extremely well. There was warmth or love and I was not lonely. I was young and beautiful. What else do I want? Especially, no more pain.

"Suddenly a nurse stood in the doorway (I was watching from above.) She glanced at that body, rushed to her, got all excited. She tried to feel the pulse, lifted the hand and let it drop. She did this three or four times. Then she ran out of the room and there was such excitement! A doctor with his stethoscope and two nurses rushed in. 'No heart beat; hurry and get an ___ injection' (I forgot the name). I was trying to tell them, 'See, I'm alive.'

"They did not answer and acted as if they did not hear or see. (This is when I noticed that my mouth did not move and I spoke loudly in thought.)

"By now I had enough of them and said 'I want to . . .' but never finished the sentence. I was interrupted by a powerful but kind voice saying, 'No, no, you must return. This is not your time.'

"Oh, no, I'm not going to return to that painful, old body. Maybe if I hurry I can. . . . Again the voice spoke, 'No, you must return or they will pronounce you dead and this is not your time.'

"Better obey" I thought, and the next moment I remembered when my soul was above the waistline of my body my eyes opened very slightly. The doctor said, 'Look, her skin is getting pink. There is a slight heartbeat.'

"Again, 'Look, she's getting more color and her heartbeat is getting stronger.' When the soul reached the top of my head, I opened my eyes wide and moved my hand. The doctor said with a smile, 'You're doing just fine. You'll be all right.' And they left."

A great many similar experiences could be mentioned, but we will proceed to other aspects of what is seen or what happens immediately after one dies.

Veil

A number of persons, both among those who died and revived and some who had visions, spoke of a "veil" through which they could see but were unable to pass into the next world. A very close friend who had several experiences of this kind told me recently, in awed voice, of the night in which he felt he was dying. He came to this veil and longed to pass through to the glory he saw beyond, but was told it was not his time. He returned to life, aglow with the presence of God.

Tunnel

Others have spoken of a passageway. Julia Ruopp said that she started down "what seemed to be a long, dark passageway."

The *Pentecostal Evangel* for November 30, 1975, contained an account of Otis G. Jones who was dying of a heart problem. He said "I seemed to be in a long corridor walking toward a door at its end. I looked up and saw in the doorway a brilliant light and a Figure." When the voice spoke to him, he was healed and returned to life.

Angels

Quite a few of those who died and returned to life, or who actually died and related at the moment of passing what they had seen, spoke of angels coming for them.

The scriptures say that when the beggar died, angels carried him to Abraham's bosom (Luke 16:19-31). In another chapter we will discuss angels in more detail. Here, however, we are only mentioning their mission of conveying to heaven the spirits of the blessed dead.

When Marietta Davis lay in a trance, she was met by an angel who conducted her spirit to the realms above. Mrs. Woodworth-Etter, an evangelist well known in bygone days, said that when a certain man whom she knew was dying, he declared that angels and his predeceased children were in the room. A tract entitled "A Wesleyan Lady," by Robert Young tells about a dying missionary lying in a trance for a week, then returning to life. She said a celestial being conducted her to the next world where she saw many whom she knew and where she heard beautiful music.

In his book about angels, Billy Graham also speaks of those who were dying and who saw angels. Elizabeth

Bossert and General Booth of the Salvation Army tell of seeing saints and angels. A close elderly friend, Mrs. Martha Legett, when she was dying, said the room was full of angels. She was surprised that others could not see them also.

Seeing the Predeceased

Besides being greeted by angels, many saw relatives who had died. Both Drs. Kubler-Ross and Moody mentioned that many of those they had interviewed reported that they had been greeted by one or more persons who had previously died.

These reports have generally been attributed to the feverish hallucinations which presumably accompany death. But Dr. Kubler-Ross replies that it could not be because when she asked five-or six-year-olds who reported this experience, who it was they saw, not one said it was mommy or daddy. It was always instead a person who had died (*Chicago Tribune*, May 23, 1976).

In the *Chicago Tribune* (May 23, 1976) Dr. Charles Garfield was quoted as saying, "A number did talk about a kind of blissful detachment from the whole process. A number said they heard celestial music. A number said they had out-of-body experiences when they dropped out of the physical boundaries of their body and watched the drama from a different perspective."

He continued: "I've heard talk of reunions, being freed, mentioning names of dead relatives. I wish I could conclude what I'd like to—that they were having some contact [with the relatives]. But right now, I'm stuck with the words."

Even some evangelical Christians who find this hard to believe are almost compelled to accept these experiences since they are too numerous to doubt, and since recently the secular world has been making concessions to the possibility of such events.

When evangelist D. L. Moody was dying, he cried, "I have been within the gates and saw the children, Dwight and Irene" (grandchildren who had died).

General Booth, founder of the Salvation Army, saw many angels and saints. He also described a celestial being as being at the same time "human, yet angelic," in his beauty. He was a friend who had died a number of years before.

In her book *To Live Again* Catherine Marshall tells of a woman who had been screaming because she didn't want to die and was given a hypo injection which put her out for seven hours. When she came to, she apologized for her previous conduct and said "Everything's all right now. I've seen Dad. He came and told me there's nothing to be afraid of. He promised that he'd stay with me every minute and hold my hand. Don't worry about me. I'm all right now." That night she died with a smile on her face, one hand outstretched (New York: McGraw-Hill, 1957, p. 170).

The father of an acquaintance of mine, Mr. Axel Hanson of Chicago, Illinois, died on August 12, 1975. His grandson, Steve Nelson, aged twelve, whom I knew well, had died six months before. During the last days of the old grandfather, he (the grandfather) talked to his deceased sister. Three days before his death, as he was lying in bed very weak, he suddenly sat up and said, "Steve, is that you, Steve?" And he began to cry. His frightened wife called out, "Dad, where are you? Come back." Mr. Hanson sank back and sobbed, "Why did you call me back. I just talked to Steve." Shortly afterward he said, "There is rejoicing . . . Father, take me home." And he died.

Another friend, Mrs. Estelle Dykstra, of Chicago, told me of the experience of her husband who died on June 21, 1955. During his last days he seemed to go into a trance and sometimes would talk to someone invisible to her. One day his face glowed and he talked and laughed saying, "Oh, I'm so glad to see you, Charlie." His wife said her husband was talking and shaking hands with someone she could not see.

Mrs. Dykstra said, "I could hear him talking to Charlie Niedzgowski but couldn't hear the answers he got from the other side." The strange thing was that as far as she knew, Charlie—who used to live in Chicago, where the Dykstras lived before moving out of state—was still living. But during her husband's funeral, which was held in Chicago, Mrs. Niedzgowski, who was present, said that her husband had died six months before.

Just before Mr. Dykstra died, his wife and the nurse saw hovering over him a substance like a cloud. She thought it was just smoke with the sun shining through. But when her husband drew his last breath, the cloud disappeared.

The following accounts appear in Chapter 16 of *The Power of Positive Thinking* by Norman Vincent Peale (New York: Prentice-Hall, 1952) and are used by permission:

A famous neurologist tells of a dying man who began to call off names, which the physician wrote down. Later he asked the daughter who they were. She replied they were all relatives who had died a long time ago. The physician said he believed his patient did see them.

Mr. and Mrs. William Sage are friends of Dr. Peale. Mr. Sage died first. A few years later when Mrs. Sage was on her deathbed, the most surprised look passed across her face and it lighted up with a wonderful smile as she called her husband's name.

Natalie Kalmus tells what happened when her sister Eleanor was dying. "Natalie," Eleanor said, "there are so many of them. There's Fred and Ruth . . . What's she doing here? Oh, I know." An electric shock went through me. She had said "Ruth" [her cousin] was here because she had died suddenly the week before, but Eleanor had not been told this.

Incidents like these have occurred so often and with such

similarity that many will find it easier to believe than to doubt them. I believe that as research by doctors, psychologists and scientists continues, enough evidence will be accumulated to cause many to reevaluate their previous negative attitudes.

CHAPTER 5

The Appointed Time

"Man's a vapor and full of woes;
Cuts a caper and away he goes."

Que sera, sera—whatever will be, will be.

Some years ago this was a popular tune. It conveyed the fatalist philosophy that whatever is destined for man will happen and that he can do nothing about it.

Is that what the Bible means when it implies that the time for our death is already determined?

Study the following scriptures to draw your own conclusions.

Is there not an appointed time to man upon earth? (Job 7.1)

. . . all the days of my appointed time will I wait till my change come. (Job 14:14)

Seeing his days are determined, the number of his months are with thee, thou hast appointed his bounds that he cannot pass. (Job 14:5)

. . . having definitely determined [their] allotted periods of time. . . . (Acts 17:26 TAB)

And when thy days be fulfilled, and thou shalt sleep with thy fathers . . . (2 Sam. 7:12)

Your eyes saw my unformed substance, and in Your book all the days of my life were written, before ever they took shape, when as yet there was none of them. (Ps. 139:16, TAB)

These scriptures seem to indicate that to each man is allotted a specific life span and that when those days are fulfilled, even to the number of months, God will terminate them.

Must we conclude then that God arbitrarily decides: "On July 10, 1986, John Jones will die?" Or does John Jones have something to say about it?

A study of the context of the promise in Exodus 23:26 ". . . the number of thy days will I fulfill," suggests that it could be conditioned upon obedience to God. Ecclesiastes 7:17 tells us "Be not over much wicked, neither be thou foolish, why shouldst thou die before thy time?" Does this mean that foolish, as well as wicked conduct could make God cut us off prematurely?

Or does God just wait until we are ready?

An old Russian proverb says "Death does not take the old, but the ripe." A gardener picks his fruit neither when it is green nor when it begins to decay, but at the fullest peak of the ripeness of which it is capable.

Just what determines the precise time when the Divine Gardener picks His fruit?

Abijah, son of wicked King Jeroboam, became very sick

(1 Kings 14:1-16). The prophet said the child would die. "He only of Jeroboam shall come to the grave, for in him there is found some good thing toward the Lord God of Israel in the house of Jeroboam" (v. 13).

Why did God's kindness take Abijah to heaven? What was this "good thing toward the Lord" which so pleased God? The Jamieson, Faucet and Brown Commentary explains on page 223: "The reason of the profound regret shown at his [Abijah's] death arose, according to Jewish writers, from his being decidedly opposed to the erection of the golden calves and using his influence with his father to allow his subjects the free privilege of going to worship in Jerusalem." He was the only one of Jeroboam's family "who should receive the rites of sepulture."

To me, this passage indicates that God determined the time of this young man's death based upon the highest degree of spiritual growth to which he would ever attain. Had Abijah taken the throne after his father's death, he likely would have gone the way of the wicked line of Jeroboam.

Consider also the story of the disobedient man of God in 1 Kings 13. This man was sent to cry against the altar of Jeroboam and was directed by God to immediately return home when his mission was completed. However, another prophet lied to him and enticed him to disobey God's order. For this disobedience the man of God lost his life.

In the light of scripture, did God arbitrarily determine the time of this prophet's death or did the prophet shorten his own life by his disobedience? Did God foresee that if this prophet had continued in the downward trend, that he would have eventually lost his reward?

I have often wondered about five well-known evangelists whom I observed over a period of years. They all had outstanding ministries of salvation and healing. And, in turn, each of them seemed to reach a place in their lives where their ministries began to deteriorate. Two of them were repeatedly told by admirers that they were Elijah, until they began to believe it. Each of these evangelists died far under their normally allotted three score and ten years.

Luke 13:6-9 contains a thought-provoking story. A certain man had a fig tree which after three years was still not producing fruit. So he told the gardner ". . . cut it down, why cumbereth it the ground?" But the gardener begged the master to try one more year of fertilizing and special care and then if it bear fruit well; and if not, he would cut it down.

Another scripture to make you think is the one found in John 15:2, "Every branch in me that beareth not fruit he taketh away. . . ." A branch in Christ must surely refer to a Christian. But here Jesus is saying that He cuts off the unfruitful branch.

Could these scriptures apply to those five evangelists who died prematurely?

I wonder if this might be the case: A child of God, of whatever chronological age, reaches a place at which he achieves his highest spiritual potential. Thereafter he begins a steady decline, from which God in His foreknowledge knows he will never recover. Would God then take that person?

If it is true that God takes us when we are ripe, we might wonder just what constitutes ripeness. Recently I spoke to a friend who had been seriously ill, and recovered. She said, "I didn't die because my work on earth was not finished. God has something more for me to do."

This is a common concept, but I believe we miss the whole point. The real factor which determines when we are ready to die is not primarily when we have finished our work for God, but rather when He has finished His work in us.

From a practical standpoint, several scriptures seem to

rather clearly promise longer life if we fulfill certain conditions.

1. Those who follow the wisdom of God will have their days and years of life increased (Prov. 3:16).

2. Length of days is promised to those who keep the law (Prov. 3:1-2).

3. The fear of the Lord will prolong our days (Prov. 10:27).

4. The New Testament promises that if we honor our parents our days will be long upon the earth (Eph. 6:2-3).

We can prolong our lives by right living: "My son, forget not my law; but let thine heart keep my commandments. For length of days, and long life, and peace, shall they add to thee" (Prov. 3:1-2).

The Amplified Version says: "For length of days, and years of a life [worth living], and tranquility [inward and outward and continuing through old age till death], these shall they add to you."

In the Book of Proverbs there are laws of good health, that is, laws of eating, laws for peace of mind, for good relationships with others. All these actually are rules for good mental and physical health. It is significant that these two are among the rules for prolonging life which are mentioned in the bulletins of the American Heart Association.

In their papers, the Heart Association says that heart disease has become the number one killer in the United States, causing over a million deaths annually.

High blood pressure is one of the chief causes of death and this disease is associated with improper eating and living patterns, including stress and tension. So observing the common sense laws of living mentioned in the Book of Proverbs would be one natural way of prolonging our days.

Therefore we can cause God to shorten our lives by what

we do spiritually and we can cause premature death by wrong living habits.

God does have a set time for each of us to die—a course marked out. For most of us, it appears that He intends that we continue in Christian service as long as possible, that we continue growing spiritually until we have reached our highest potential, and that we die at a truly ripe old age.

Our times are in His hands and those hands are very capable and accustomed to functioning only in the greatest love and wisdom, in relation to our temporal and our eternal good. He can be trusted to take us to himself at the best possible time.

CHAPTER 6

The Spirit Form

The spirit form—that part of man which upon death leaves the body—what is it like?

During childhood we avoided walking past a cemetery at night, just in case it might be haunted by ghosts, one of whom might stealthily creep from behind a tall tombstone and holler "Boo!" Dramatized by cartoonists featuring spooks hovering over graves at Halloween, these scary images may be carried over into our more rational years. When we became Christians we lost our eerie feelings about death and everything associated with it, but often retained that disturbing sense of mystery.

Except what we learn by inference, we do not find in the Bible much specific and direct information about the form and characteristics of the soul. We can, however, refer to two passages which speak in a generalized way of two kinds of after-death forms:

Paul spoke of the resurrection body (1 Cor. 15) and, in general terms, the spirit body (2 Cor. 5).

The Resurrection Body

Before we discuss the subject of this chapter—the spirit

body—we will talk a little about the resurrection body. The latter is of course the more important, since it is the body in which all Christians will eventually live throughout eternity.

Jesus died, was resurrected and ascended into heaven in a glorified physical body. At the Second Coming of Christ the bodies of the dead in Christ, rising from graves, will be reunited with their spirits (which had already been in heaven); and the bodies of living saints will be changed into immortal bodies; and all will return with Jesus to heaven in glorified, physical bodies of flesh and bone like His (1 Thess. 4:15-17; 1 Cor. 15:51-54).

What will this resurrection body be like?

We can assume it will be like the body of Jesus after His resurrection. In this body He was seen and touched; He ate and talked to His disciples. To demonstrate the substance of His body, Jesus said "Behold my hands and my feet, that it is I myself; handle me, and see; for a spirit hath not flesh and bones, as ye see me have" (Luke 24:39).

Yet in this same body Jesus was able to pass through closed doors, to appear and disappear, to transport himself from place to place and finally to ascend into heaven.

John Bunyan, during his vision, was informed concerning this glorified body: It is a "body rarified from all gross alloys of corruption and made a pure and refined body and yet a substantial one, not composed of wind and air as mortals below are apt to imagine" (*Visions*, p. 26).

This gives us an idea of what the Apostle Paul meant when he said "There is a natural body and there is a spiritual body" (1 Cor. 15:44). The context in this chapter of scripture lets us know he was speaking of the resurrection body.

The Spirit Body
Up until the time of the resurrection, there will be

multitudes of saints in heaven in spirit bodies. What is this body like?

We find in 2 Corinthians 5:1-8 the nearest to any Bible description of this form. The King James Version says that when our earthly house is dissolved, we will be clothed upon with our heavenly house, "If so be that being clothed, *we shall not be found naked*" (v.3, italics mine).

The Living Bible Version expresses it like this:

"For we know that when this tent we live in now is taken down—when we die and leave these bodies—we will have wonderful *new bodies* in heaven, homes that will be ours forevermore, made for us by God himself, and not by human hands. . . . That is why we look forward eagerly to the day when we shall have heavenly bodies, which we shall put on like new clothes. *For we shall not be merely spirits without bodies.* These earthly bodies make us groan and sigh, but we wouldn't like to think of dying and having *no bodies at all.* We want to slip into our *new bodies* so that these dying bodies will, as it were, be swallowed up by everlasting life. This is what God has prepared for us and, as a guarantee, he has given us his Holy Spirit" (2 Cor. 5:1-5, italics mine).

So, "the naked spirit" will receive some kind of body. However, this passage does not describe it. Is it visible or invisible? Can it be touched and felt? Is it ghostly and vaporous or does it have human form? Is it identifiable as the person who once lived in the mortal body?

Generally speaking, a spirit is invisible—whether it be the Spirit of God or of an angel (who is called a ministering spirit) or the spirit of a deceased person. Except for the times when "the Lord opens the eyes," a spirit is invisible to a mortal. However, a spirit is able not only to see other spirits, but also mortal beings.

We can better understand the nature of the spirit form by examining scripture passages pertaining to angels.

Although spirit beings, they frequently appeared in a visible form to various Old and New Testament characters, exhibiting characteristics of human personality.

Jacob saw angels, Gideon spoke to one, so did Abraham. When the angel appeared to Mary she both saw him and heard him speak in an audible voice. When Peter was in prison the angel "smote" him on the side with such force that he awoke, therefore there was some kind of impact that could be felt.

Since scripture gives no specific word about the appearance of the spirit form of the deceased, we can conclude from the above that this form is likely to possess properties both human and angelic.

Because God has promised to speak to His children through dreams and visions in the latter days, He has through these means given us sources of further information.

During his vision of heaven, General Booth tells that he saw a celestial being who was a redeemed one, of whom the general said, "I could never have believed the human face divine to bear so grand a stamp of dignity and charm" (*Visions*, p. 19).

When Singh was taken to heaven, he conversed with a man who was describing the appearance of his spirit as he examined it at the moment of death: "Then he examined his spiritual body and found it beautifully light and delicate and totally different from his gross material body" (*Visions*, p. 25).

John Bunyan described a certain deceased saint whom he saw during his vision: "I saw coming toward me a glorious appearance, like the appearance of a man, but circled round about with beams of inexpressible light and glory which streamed from him all the way he came" (*Visions*, p. 8).

(One is reminded of the passage, "And they that be wise

shall shine as the brightness of the firmament; and they that turn many to righteousness as the stars forever and ever" [Dan. 12:3]).

Another celestial being explained that his shining beams were but reflections of the glory of Jesus, whose presence was all around (*ibid.*).

Bunyan wrote, "A shining form drew near. It was one of the redeemed. He told me that he had left his body below, resting in hope until the resurrection; and that *though he was still a substance, yet it was an immaterial one, not to be touched by mortals*" (p. 29, italics mine).

Marietta Davis, during her trance in which she was taken to heaven, made some of the most detailed and profound observations concerning the state of the dead. She said that while she was in heaven, she was instructed about old and familiar friends whom she had met there.

"Although I knew them, their appearance was unlike that while upon earth, each being an embodiment of intellect unassociated with the physical form in which I had known them before. Not having power or any means adapted to convey a just idea, I can only give feeble utterance to my conceptions of their nature by saying they appeared all mind, all light, all glory, all adoration, all love supremely pure, all peace and calm serenity, all united in sublime employ, all expression of heavenly unfolding joy" (*Scenes*, p. 26).

And yet, though they appeared in such a spiritual form, she was able to recognize and to embrace and to be embraced by friends and to freely communicate with them.

The most recent findings concerning the spirit form are those of Dr. Elisabeth Kubler-Ross, Dr. Raymond Moody and others mentioned in the newspaper articles. (These mainly concern persons who died and were revived.)

In the October 16, 1975, *Tribune* article Dr. Kubler-Ross

says of the spirit body, "They have a fabulous feeling of peace and wholeness. People who are blind can see, paraplegics have legs they can move. They have no pain, no fear, no anxiety."

One of the first sensations experienced by many was weightlessness and a great freedom from the encumbrance of their bodies. They could see much more clearly and at greater distances, their minds were more acute, they could hear with clarity previously unknown to themselves, and their mental perceptions had increased.

My friend, whose letter I recorded anonymously earlier, says that when she saw her own body she had arms, legs, face and her own personality; she could see, hear, think, was younger and free from pain. Her various faculties were improved.

From the story of Lazarus recorded in Luke 16:19-31 we can infer that the spirit form will be recognizable as the same person in whose body he once resided.

Among those who had out-of-body experiences, many felt so much themselves that they had no idea they were dead. In speaking of his spirit body, no one has ever referred to it as "my spirit," but as "myself." Various ones have said "I looked down and saw what was happening in the operating room." Or, "I felt light and weightless." Or, "I had no pain." Or, "I was extremely happy and well."

Always it was "I" and not "my spirit."

Summing up the experiences in scripture and the varied experiences of those having visions and the like, we can say: The spirit has a body, but of a very different nature and with different powers. Though it is invisible to mortals and is able to pass through solid objects, yet the spirit has characteristics we commonly associate with the body. The spirit can see, hear, move, think; it is young, full of vigor, without pain, whole and happy beyond belief.

The Spirit Form

Scripture tells us that man is composed of an invisible, immaterial spirit and soul, living in a visible, material body. The real person is not the mortal, corruptible body, but the immortal spirit living within it. Because we are usually more aware of body than soul, this spirit being or person seems unreal and mysterious to us.

But "the house which is from heaven," the spiritual body, is not vaporous but is very real and very wonderful. Those who have never experienced the separation of the two elements find it impossible to describe or understand what it is like. And it is in this form that we will live happily in heaven until the time of the resurrection, when spirit and body will again be joined to form a new glorified, immortal body.

CHAPTER 7

Paradise

While the ambulance screamed the warning of its approach toward the hospital, Bill writhed on the cot inside clutching at his heart. Between gasps of pain he prayed, "Oh, God, you helped me before, help me now. I'm ready, but Mary needs me." By the time he was wheeled into the emergency room, Bill was unconscious.

When he again opened his eyes, he looked around with amazed delight.

He and Mary had vacationed in many beautiful places—among the giant redwoods of California, the blue lakes of Canada, the flamboyant flowers and birds of Florida, the multicolored canyons of the Southwest. But never had he seen beauty like this: trees and mountains more majestic, lakes clearer and bluer, flowers more vividly hued. The very atmosphere was different. He seemed surrounded by love, and filled with it. Never before had he felt such complete joy and peace and acceptance. Where could he be? Surely he wasn't dreaming. Everything was too real.

In the distance he now saw an intensely brilliant light; no, the light was not in the distance, it was here, it was everywhere, but seemed concentrated beyond. And in that direction he was irresistibly drawn.

Often he had enjoyed the living, pulsating presence of God, but this Presence was so powerful, it was almost more than he could bear.

Then he saw coming toward him his father, his mother, his brother Pete—hands extended, smiling the sweetest of smiles. Something about them was different. And suddenly Bill *knew*.

His parents had died years before, his brother just three months ago. "I must be dead," Bill thought; "I must be in heaven. I—I—don't understand. My body is down there, yet this spirit form is so real, so wonderful. This is me; I am myself.

"I can't wait to tell Mary, she won't worry about me any more. No, I can't tell her now. She's on earth, I'm in heaven."

His sorrow was swallowed up in the magnitude of the marvels around him, and in the glory of that immense love which flowed from the great light shining, distant, yet close—encompassing everything and everyone in its warm embrace.

This story, of course, is fantasy; but not really. For what the hypothetical Bill experienced and saw has been experienced and seen by many who were taken into heaven or granted visions of heaven.

As mentioned in Chapter 3, the word heaven is used in scripture in three ways: The first heaven refers to the atmosphere surrounding our earth; the second heaven to the region of planets and stars, and the third heaven to God's dwelling.

The place at which the blessed dead arrive is called by the Apostle Paul both heaven and paradise (2 Cor. 12:1-4). The "overcomer" was promised that he would "eat of the tree of life, which is in the midst of the paradise of God" (Rev. 2:7); and to the thief who repented on the cross, Jesus promised "To day shalt thou be with me in paradise" (Luke 23:43). Paul said also that when we are absent from the body we are present with the Lord (2 Cor. 5:8). The Lord is, of course, in heaven.

Therefore, the moment a person dies and leaves his body, he moves to another realm. We have noticed in Chapter 4 that there may be an interval immediately after death when the soul hovers over his body or remains on earth for a time. But whatever the interval, the next thing that happens is that he is present with the Lord, or in paradise.

When Lazarus died, the scripture says he was carried by the angels into Abraham's bosom (Luke 16:22). This tells us that souls are accompanied by at least one angelic guide. We know further, from visions, that they often are accompanied by friends or relatives and sometimes by the Lord Jesus himself.

There is a good reason why the soul needs an angelic escort, for after passing through the first heaven or the atmosphere, there remains a dangerous area to traverse.

Satan is called "The prince of the power of the air" (Eph. 2:2). And "We wrestle against . . . the rulers of the darkness of this world, against wicked spirits in high [heavenly] places" (Eph. 6:12).

Somewhere between earth's atmosphere and the third heaven is the domain of Satan and his hosts. Billy Graham in his book, *Angels, God's Secret Messengers*, says, "Death is robbed of much of its terror for the true believer, but we still need God's protection as we take that last journey. At the moment of death the spirit departs from the body and moves through the atmosphere. But the Scripture teaches us that the devil lurks there. He is 'the Prince of the power of the air' (Eph. 2:2). If the eyes of our understanding were opened, we would probably see the air filled with demons, the enemies of Christ. If Satan could hinder the angel of Daniel for three weeks on his mission to earth, we can imagine the opposition a Christian may encounter at death.

"But Christ on Calvary cleared a road through Satan's kingdom. When Christ came to earth, He had to pass through the devil's territory and open up a beachhead here. That is one reason He was accompanied by a host of angels when He came (Luke 2:8-14). And this is why holy angels will accompany Him when He comes again (Matt. 16:27). Till then, the moment of death is Satan's final opportunity to attack the true believer; but God has sent His angels to guard us at that time" (New York: Doubleday, 1975, by permission, pp. 150-151).

When John Bunyan was taken to heaven, in vision as he rose higher, the earth below appeared to him as a little dark spot. Upon inquiring about it, his guide told him it was earth. Bunyan then asked "What were those multitudes of black and horrid forms that hover in the air above the world?" The angel replied that they were fallen and apostate spirits "which for their pride and rebellion were cast down from heaven and wander in the air by the decree of the Almighty . . . from thence they are permitted to descend into the world, both for the trial of the elect and for the condemnation of the wicked" (*Visions*, p. 12).

After Elisabeth Bossert had been in heaven for a time, the Lord told her to look down and she said "As I looked down, down, past the clouds, fog and mist, I saw this earth which looked like a little ball. It was swarming thick with devils about it. I never realized there were so many devils as that down on the earth from which I came" (*My Visit*, p. 15).

Having been safely conducted through Satan's domain, as souls approached paradise, their experiences were varied.

Many first saw a bright light which grew in intensity and

beauty as they came nearer; others heard rapturous music, both vocal or instrumental. Some had glimpses of a dazzlingly beautiful city, or passed through magnificent gates; many saw scenes of nature far lovelier than anything they had ever beheld on earth.

What actually happens on arrival in paradise? The Scripture makes the simple and very broad statement that we will be with Jesus (Luke 23:43; 2 Cor. 5:8). Further details are supplied by those who were granted experiences of heaven.

In the smallness and personalness of our concepts, we are apt to think of newcomers arriving singly. But if we realized that about 1,910,000 people died in 1975 in the United States alone (*World Almanac and Book of Facts*, 1977), and that many of them were Christians, we would understand that the reception area of heaven is a very busy place.

Sadhu Singh says, "I saw that from all sides thousands upon thousands of souls were constantly arriving in the world of spirits and that all were attended by angels" (*Visions*, p. 10).

Having arrived, what is the reaction of the person who like "Bill" did not expect to die, but suddenly finds himself in a spirit body in heaven?

Several whose experiences were studied mentioned the surprise of those who suddenly died.

Singh says "Death comes so suddenly to many that it is only with great difficulty that they realize that they have left behind the material world and entered this world of spirits.

"Bewildered by the many new things that they see around them, they imagine that they are visiting some country or city of the physical world, which they had not seen before. It is only when they have been more fully instructed and realize that their spiritual body is different from their former material body, that they allow that they have in fact

51

been transferred from the material world to the realm of spirits" (p. 8).

When she saw souls newly arriving in paradise, Miss Davis asked her guide about it. He replied, "These beings moving about thee, once the inhabitants of earth whence thou art, having left their mortal dwellings, are commencing a new state of existence. Their surprise is the effect of their sudden change from external objects and sense to spiritual, and their more immediate knowledge of cause and effect" (*Scenes*, p. 21).

Since many, like Peter Marshall, die suddenly of heart attacks, when that person finds himself in heaven, a period of adjustment is often necessary. Mrs. Marshall, in writing about her husband, said that moments after his death, her husband was still the same person he had been before his death, except that he had "shed his physical body," and that he was allowed to work in the garden to give him time to recover from his bewilderment over his own death (*To Live Again*, p. 24).

But we believe that whatever the preliminary reaction the newly arrived person may have, he will eventually become completely happy. For the scripture says "And God shall wipe away all tears from their eyes . . ." (Rev. 21:4).

Sadhu Singh notes "On entering the world of spirits, he at once feels at home, for not only are his friends about him but while in the world, he had been preparing himself for that home by his trust in God and fellowship with Him. . . ."

He adds "As a child born into the world finds everything provided for its wants, so does the soul on entering the spiritual world find all his wants supplied" (*Visions*, p. 10).

Having been welcomed and having adjusted to the surprise and realization of being in heaven, what then?

We must remember that souls arrive in paradise in greatly different spiritual states—from the newly converted, uncivilized heathen to the college-educated old saint who had for many years served God. Obviously each would be happiest with others who are on their own spiritual levels.

Miss Davis said that "All classes as they emerge from the physical form are attracted to and mingle with kindred associations, beings to whose character they assimilate" (*Scenes*, p. 20).

"After death," according to Sadhu Singh, "the soul of every human being will enter the world of spirits and every one, according to the state of spiritual growth, will dwell with spirits like in mind and in nature to himself. . . . Usually Christ reveals himself in the spiritual world to each one in the degrees of glory differing in intensity according to the state of each soul's spiritual development" (*Visions*, p. 10).

But the glory, even of the blessed dead, is so great that it is almost more than the newly arrived can bear. So it must take a period before he is able to look upon Him in His fullness; so He decreases His gllory to accommodate the ability of that newcomer to behold Jesus.

Whatever the spiritual state of the newly arrived person, and for whatever part of paradise he will be fitted, he will find his new environment exceedingly beautiful. In the concordance located in the back of my King James Bible there is this note: "Paradise. Probably a Persian word signifying a park and used by the LXX [Septuagint, an ancient Greek translation of the Old Testament] as a translation of the Hebrew Eden. It is used as a symbol of the region of heavenly blessedness."

In his booklet "A Citizen of Two Worlds," Gordon Lindsay explains that "heaven in many ways will correspond with what we are familiar on earth, except that it will be purer, more perfect and free from the curse of sin."

Revelation 22:1-2 mentions a river and the tree of life as being a part of heaven. Some translations mention trees in the plural.

Why should it be hard for us to believe that paradise is a place as real and as tangible as the garden of Eden? It must be prepared in such a way as to accommodate the final form of man, which will be a physical, but glorified body of flesh and bones.

And why should we find it hard to believe that in paradise there will be eating; for Jesus in His glorified body ate in the presence of His disciples. We must remember that when God first made man and put him in the garden of Eden, that God intended that man should never die but remain there in a physical, incorruptible body.

Should it be surprising that God would restore man to be what He originally intended him to be—a physical but spiritual being, living in a material but spiritual paradise?

In the visions of those who saw heaven or were taken there, paradise was always a real place.

During her experience of seeing a part of heaven, Julia Ruopp spoke of seeing children singing and frolicking in an apple orchard. She said "The air had a brilliant clarity that made small details stand out in a new light; the orchard in translucent white and pinks, startling shades of greens, reds, yellows and russets—for there were both fragrant blossoms and ripe red fruits on the trees" (*Window of Heaven*, p. 29).

Ivan Moiseyev was a young Russian soldier who was persecuted and, eventually, tortured and murdered by the secret police for his Christian testimony, which they considered anti-Soviet. His poignant story is told for English readers by Myrna Grant in her book, *Vanya* (Carol Stream, Illinois: Creation House, 1974). God wonderfully supported Ivan during his ordeal. The young man received frequent visions and sometimes even experienced miracles. On one occasion, according to Ms. Grant, he was awakened from a peaceful sleep by an angel who escorted him on a vision of heaven. "In the brilliance of this world, every detail of blade of grass and petal of flower stood out as if floodlit. The patterns of the bark upon the trees were indescribably beautiful. The expanse of the branches were profoundly graceful, so luminous that the light seemed to pour from within each tree. Instinctively Ivan lifted his eyes to the sky, gazing in every direction. There was no sun" (p. 63).

In his book, Sadhu Singh writes: "In every part of heaven there are superb gardens which all the time produce every variety of sweet and luscious fruit and all kinds of sweet scented flowers that never fade. In them creatures of every kind give praise to God unceasingly. Birds, beautiful in hue, raise their sweet songs of praise and such is the singing of angels and saints that on hearing their songs a wonderful sense of rapture is experienced.

"Wherever one may look there is nothing but scenes of unbounded joy. This in truth is the paradise that God has prepared for those that love Him, where there is no shade of death nor error, nor sin, nor suffering but abiding peace and joy" (*Visions*, p. 26).

The vision of Marietta Davis was to a great extent about what happens to children and infants who die. Here she describes the part of paradise to which children go:

"Soon we entered a plain whereon were visible trees, bearing fruit. Passing through these shadowy groves, I was delighted with the melody of the birds, whose warbling notes arose in sweetest song. There we paused. Supposing that I was on some terrestrial orb, I inquired of its name.

"My guide answered 'These trees, these flowers, these birds occupy the outer expanse of the spiritual Paradise. So pure are they and so refined that mortals with beclouded vision may not behold them. And so soft their notes that they are not made audible to the dull hearing of men. Beings inhabiting forms more gross do not conceive the reality of the existence of nature so refined. Absent from the body, you can comprehend through spiritual senses the existence and reality of spiritual habitations; but what you now behold is but the outline and more exterior [part] of the home of spirits. These floral plains and warbling melodies are but the lower order of the external habitation of the sanctified.

" 'Here the redeemed are first conducted by their guardian protectors as they leave the valley and shadow of death and here they are taught the rudiments of immortal life. . . . Here friends who have advanced in spiritual attainments return from higher employment to welcome the spirit on its entrance upon this plane of the spirit world. Here kindred are permitted to meet and hold converse; and it is in these immortal groves where spirits first attempt in unity the song of redeeming grace and reposing in soft and heavenly sweetness, breathe the pure air of Paradise' " (*Scenes*, p. 22).

If all of this seems too wonderful to believe, remember, the scripture says "Eye hath not seen nor ear heard, neither have entered into the heart of man the things which God hath prepared for them that love him" (1 Cor. 2:9).

CHAPTER 8

The City of God

Laboriously, the old man shuffled down a rocky path, stumbling over the uneven ground, carefully stepping around embedded stones. As he approached the beach, he pulled his faded cloak around his bony frame, shivering in the early morning breeze. He made his way to his favorite rock, formed somewhat like a chair. As he gazed at the tranquil waters, rays of the rising sun filtered through his white hair, making it look like a halo, framing his saintly face.

With serene eyes, blue as the sea, he followed the flight of a large bird, turning his head toward the old shack he called home. He didn't mind its sparse furnishings—a bed, chair, table—the most important to him being the table which held his parchments and writing material.

Above the crudely made chest which stored his few possessions, he had hung a device for marking the passage of time.

So he knew that it was the Lord's day—though it seemed to him that every day was God's. Still, he made special note of the first day of the week, remembering the joyful fellowship he used to have with Christian friends before he was forced to come to this island.

As he lifted his head and his heart in worship, he suddenly heard behind him a commanding sound, like the blare of a trumpet. Turning, he beheld a glorious, radiant figure, from whom flowed blinding rays of light. As he continued to stare, he realized that it was his Lord!

And John, exiled to the Isle of Patmos, fell at His feet as dead.

From this moment on, John, while in the spirit, received a series of revelations which are now recorded in the last book of the Bible. For twenty chapters he writes of what is and what is to come, and in the last two chapters he records his visions of heaven. "And I John saw the holy city, New Jerusalem, coming down from God out of heaven, prepared as a bride adorned for her husband" (Rev. 21:2).

So now we will talk about this magnificent place, the eternal home of God's children. The Holy City is not of course heaven itself, but a part of it; because the scripture says John saw the holy city come down *out of* heaven.

Much has been written about the order of events before and after the descent of the New Jerusalem. Most people agree that the coming of Jesus will be the time of the resurrection, when bodies and souls of the dead will be reunited, and when bodies of the living will put on immortality. Somewhere between this coming and the closing of time, a number of events take place, the order of which scholars do not agree upon. Hence the following listing is not meant to be an arbitrary one, but simply a recording. You can place them in whatever order you or your church believes is correct:

The judgment of believers, in which they will be rewarded according to their works; the millennium; the coming of Christ to punish the wicked; the resurrection and judgment of the wicked dead; the creation of the new heavens and the new earth; the marriage supper of the Lamb, and the descent of the Holy City. (Some say it will descend to the renovated earth, others say it will be suspended above it.)

Since I am not here concerned about divergent theological viewpoints, I will simply tell about the New Jerusalem as seen by John in Revelation 21 and 22, and will also describe it as seen in supernatural experiences.

The events of the Book of Revelation were apparently seen by John both in vision and by actual transport into heaven. The first chapter speaks of John seeing Jesus. In chapter four he says, "After this I looked and behold, a door was opened in heaven" (v. 1). He then heard a voice telling him to "Come up hither and I will show thee things which must be hereafter." This sounds as though he had been taken into heaven in spirit.

If you want a good foundation for what follows, why don't you pause and read Chapters 21 and 22 of Revelation before proceeding?

Briefly, then, this is what John saw: A beautiful city, having the glory of God, surrounded by a wall made of jasper. There were twelve gates guarded by angels, each gate made of one pearl. Supporting the wall were twelve foundations made of the various semi-precious stones listed in Chapter 21.

The streets of the city were made of gold so pure that it looked like transparent glass. The measurements of the city make it a cube 1500 miles high, wide and long or 1,875,000,000 cubic miles.

In the next chapter, John tells about the throne of God, located in heaven, and about a river of life which proceeds from the throne of God, beside which is the tree of life bearing a different kind of fruit every month for twelve months.

A number of Bible teachers say believers will remain in

that part of heaven called paradise until the time of the resurrection, after which they will be transferred to the New Jerusalem. Others say paradise and the New Jerusalem are simply different sections of heaven.

Since God is so great that the heaven and the heaven of heavens cannot contain Him, it may be that His throne, the place from which He rules the universe is a separate part of heaven.

However, we know that heaven, paradise, the New Jerusalem, will be a place of perfect peace and unending happiness, not just because of the beauty all around, but chiefly because ". . . the throne of God and of the Lamb shall be in it" (Rev. 22:3).

We are devoting this chapter to describe the New Jerusalem, or the urban area of heaven, in contrast to the "rural" part of heaven—the natural beauty of paradise.

In speaking of the New Jerusalem the Bible uses these terms: A city which has foundations, whose builder and maker is God (Heb. 11:10); He hath prepared from them a city (Heb. 11:16); seek a continuing city (Heb. 13:14); the city of the living God, the heavenly Jerusalem (Heb. 12:22).

It is interesting to note that those who were either transported to heaven or had visions of it, saw its various parts—"rural" areas with trees and grass and rivers; and "urban" areas, a beautiful city with buildings and houses. But even in the city section, as in any other city, there are trees, grass, flowers and fountains, as well as temples, buildings, dwelling places or houses.

Singh tells of the beautiful buildings and homes. One man, Singh relates, who was taken to heaven said, "In the nearby houses saints like-minded to himself lived in happy fellowship" (*Visions*, p. 27).

Mrs. W.B. McKay said this regarding her vision: "The angel that was leading the way took me by the hand and led me into the city of God. I looked and my eyes beheld a wall of glittering stones, different colors beautiful beyond human conception. The large gate of pearl was wide open and the angel led me through the gate to the street of highly polished gold. There were steeples pointing upward which shone like diamonds. The angel took me by the hand and showed me a large tree laden with fruit and alongside of the tree was a river as clear as glass" (Gordon Lindsay, *True Visions of the Unseen World* [Dallas: Christ for the Nations, n.d.] pp. 34,35).

When Elizabeth Bossert was in heaven, she saw a large, beautiful gate, sparkling with splendor, beside which stood a celestial being (*My Visit*, p. 11).

Quite a number of those having visions spoke of seeing a brilliant light as they approached heaven; others also mentioned seeing or going through sparkling white gates, attended by angels.

The most detailed descriptions of parts of the heavenly city were given by Marietta Davis.

"Beneath me the sublime Temple of Instruction, builded of most precious materials and in a style of architecture which I am unable to describe, arose in the air from the center of a circular lawn of great extent, whose green surface appeared covered with the softest and richest verdure. Majestic trees in groups and at regular intervals arose, bearing a profusion of fragrant and shining clusters of flowers" (*Scenes*, p. 52).

She went on to say that the city was divided into twelve great divisions by the river and that twelve other streets intersected a spiral avenue.

These same divisons were mentioned in the H.A. Baker books as having been seen by the children of the Adullam Orphanage in China. The children, being ragged orphans from the street, knew nothing about the Book of Revelation, nor did they have imaginative powers to create such a vision, since they were mostly dull mentally.

Missionary Louisa Vaughn writes in a tract (*The Woman Who Saw God* [Randleman, North Carolina: Pilgrim Tracts Society, n.d.]) about an illiterate Chinese woman who saw the city of God. As Miss Vaughn was teaching a group of women, she said that a certain Mrs. Jang, who seemed "if possible, a little more stupid than the rest," was converted. A year and a half later Mrs. Jang lay on her death bed and said:

"I remember seeing all the family around me crying. Then the Lord came into my room and took me by the hand and said 'Come with me.' In a short time we were before a gate of pearl. It was the gate of Heaven. . . . Angels opened it and we went in and I saw many beautiful houses, all pretty colors.

"I walked beside the Lord on the golden streets. . . . Then we went on and I saw thousands of angels in a circle singing and playing lovely music. In the midst was the Throne of Glory. The heavenly Father sat upon it and when I saw Him, I was afraid. I hardly dared to lift my eyes.

" 'You have come,' He said.

"And I answered 'Yes, Lord.'

"Then He said 'You may go back for a while but you must return to Me here on the twelfth of the month.' "

When Mrs. Jang told this story to her heathen relatives and neighbors, hundreds were converted. On the twelfth of the following month, at sunset, she went back to God.

Such descriptions of the heavenly city were repeated in a very similar fashion by numbers of those whose experiences are recorded.

In May, 1976, I conversed with a woman who told me about her grandfather, Charles Norenberg. When he was dying his wife called his name. He opened his eyes and said,

"Don't call me back again. It's all white and gold and the most beautiful sight I ever saw."

When Ivan Moiseyev was taken by the angel to the other world, the angel said that because the youth was still in his body, he would have to view the New Jerusalem from another planet.

" 'We will fly together to another planet,' the angel said, 'and I will show you the light of this city, for you to know while you are yet alive in your earth body, that in certainty there is a New Jerusalem.'

"In an instant they flew to another planet where there were high mountains. Again the glory of the light illuminated every detail of this world. Ivan's eyes rested on diamond streams coursing down the mountain slopes into mists that rose from vividly green valleys. When they had come to a very deep canyon, the angel and Ivan descended until they were at the bottom.

"The angel seemed a flame of joy, the Voice more ceremonious and jubilant than Ivan had yet heard it. 'Vanya, look upward and you will see this light of the New Jerusalem.'

"At first glance Ivan recoiled in dismay. The brilliance was so intense that though he had seen it only for a second, he was sure he had been blinded. The angel spoke immediately, 'Nothing will happen to you. Look.'

"No man rescued from a desert ever drank water more thirstily than Ivan drank in the splendor of that light. So great was its power it could be felt, tasted, heard. The sight of it was not a sensation of his eyes, but of his whole being. Ivan could have wept with grief and disappointment when the angel said 'The time has come to fly back to earth' " (*Vanya*, pp. 63-64).

In August, 1959, Mrs. Betty Malz died of a ruptured appendix. Catherine Marshall wrote her story for the May,

1976, issue of *Guideposts*. The story also is in a booklet written by Mrs. Malz as well as a cassette tape (*Twenty-four Hours* [Pasadena, Texas: by author, n.d.]).

As Mrs. Malz's father stood beside her corpse repeating the name of Jesus, she said she remembers walking effortlessly to the top of a hill covered with velvety green grass, whose every blade seemed alive. Beside her was a majestic silvery-marble wall. An angel stepped forward and opened beautiful translucent pearl gates with gothic scroll at the top. When he asked if she wanted to enter, Mrs. Malz replied that she wanted to return to her family.

Looking inside the gates, she said, "I stood there and received something I can never explain. I shall never forget the majesty of the presence of God in Heaven."

When she started back down the hill, she saw a beautiful sunset rising over the marble wall, then found herself in the hospital bed, feeling the warmth of those beams. On one of these rays she saw lettered in words of ivory two inches high: "St. John 11:25, I am the resurrection and the life; he that believeth on me, though he were dead, yet shall he live."

As she reached up to touch those words, she felt the warmth pulsate through her dead body. She pushed the sheet off her face and was restored to life and perfect health.

Immediately after Marvin Ford died in January, 1972, as his spirit traveled upward, he saw "iridescent lights beckoning me into the most beautiful city I had ever seen.

"It was immense! I cannot verbalize the magnitude nor the splendor of that city. All was so overwhelmingly bright. It was like flying into Los Angeles on a smogless night at Christmas time when scintillating lights of every hue are arrayed in breathtaking magnificence. But this was magnified into a brilliancy millions of times greater than anything this planet could produce. I saw its gates of pearl, its streets of gold—not simply *paved* with gold but a solid, yet crystal-clear gold.

"I viewed its walls of jasper consisting of a heavenly green unlike anything I had ever seen before. I could see the marble-like vein running all through it. There were colors that are indescribable, for how can one describe a color without comparison to other colors? There *is no* comparison. Then I saw one resplendent light emanating from the center of the right of God's throne. I recognized it as being Jesus, my Savior! Although I did not view Him as a corporeal being, He welcomed me into His presence and I began to worship Him" ("Thirty Minutes in Heaven," *Full Gospel Business Men's Voice*, October, 1976, pp. 9,12).

After having been in heaven for thirty minutes, Mr. Ford looked down into the hospital at his own corpse and saw Rev. Ralph Wilkerson enter. As the minister rebuked death in Jesus' name and commanded the spirit to return, Mr. Ford was restored to life. He is now witnessing everywhere to the grace and power of God.

If we have found it hard to believe the vision of Marietta Davis, written over one hundred years ago, it should be easier to accept the stories in recent accounts.

To sum up all that was here written about the New Jerusalem, we can repeat the words of Thomas Edison who, just as he was dying, cried, "It is very beautiful over there" (Norman Vincent Peale, *The Power of Positive Thinking*, p. 257).

CHAPTER 9

Details about Life in Heaven

When we think of heaven, many questions occur to us. Some can be answered by scripture, others by the experiences of those who had been in heaven. For example, what language is used in heaven? Paul mentioned "the tongues of men and of angels" (1 Cor. 13:1), so we may assume that angels have a language of their own. Both Marietta Davis (*Scenes*, p. 24) and Carol Hooley (*Caught Up to Heaven* [Denver: Liberty, n.d.] pp. 5-6) heard angels converse but did not understand what they were saying. Perhaps a universal language is spoken and it may be the one used by angels.

However, when various people were taken to heaven and talked to celestial beings, it was always in his own earthly language.

Communication by Thought

Daisy Dryden, the child whose predeceased brother often visited her during her three days of dying, said, "We just talk with our think" (*Visions*, p. 23).

The anonymous friend whose letter is recorded in Chapter 4 said she communicated by thought. Several who had supernatural experiences said they communicated the same way. They also said they instinctively knew many of the various Bible saints in heaven. This should not be considered strange because 1 Corinthians 13:12 says that ". . . then I shall know even as also I am known." But whatever the means, whether vocal or mental, in heaven we will discover that "fellowship of kindred minds."

In his vision Bunyan was instructed by a celestial being, "Here we communicate the purest pleasure to each other, unfeigned ardent love uniting all our pure society. Here everyone is perfectly amiable and perfectly enamored with each other. And oh how happy is this state of love! How it doth ravish me to see my fellow saints shining with an immortal loveliness! And where there is love like this, all must be delight. And how can it be otherwise, since in this blessed society there is a continual receiving and returning of love and joy and their conversation and relationship is ravishing" (*Visions*, p. 30).

How Do They Travel in Heaven?

Since we now have sent man to the moon and placed complicated instruments on Mars, we have a better understanding of space travel. In the distant future, it may be possible for man to discover the secrets of interplanetary travel. He will still be bound, however, by human limitations. After a person leaves his body, these limitations no longer exist, for he enters a realm in which space and time are entirely different from that to which he has been accustomed on earth. In the Bible, when angels appeared to man, when Enoch and Elijah were taken to heaven, when Jesus ascended—they all must have covered the immense distance in a short time, perhaps with the speed of thought.

Visions and experiences of those who had been in heaven describe different modes of travel. Sadhu Singh tells of seeing a recently deceased mother talking with her son who had already been in heaven for a time. As they *walked* together he showed her various places of interest (*Visions*, p. 12). Others have also mentioned leisurely walking in heaven.

Since heaven is a very large place, some have wondered whether saints will be allowed to visit the various parts. One saint told Singh, "The place of residence is appointed for each soul in that plane to which his spiritual development has fitted him, but for short periods he can go to visit other spheres" *(ibid.)*.

Travel to distant places may be accomplished through instant transportation. Sadhu Singh says, "In heaven distance is never felt by anyone, for as soon as one forms the wish to go to a certain place he at once finds himself there. Distances are felt only in the material world. If one wishes to see a saint in another sphere, either he himself is transported there in a moment of thought, or at once the distant saint arrives in his presence" (*Visions*, p. 31).

When Ivan Moiseyev was taken by the angel to another planet, he said they arrived "in an instant" *(Vanya*, pp. 63-64).

So it seems that in heaven the saints both walk in the normal way for short distances, but are immediately transported when greater distances are involved.

Occupation

Another question which troubles many is "What am I going to do in heaven? Forever is a long, long time."

Vacations and periods of rest are fine, but when they extend beyond a few weeks (as in the case of convalescence or being out of work) prolonged idleness becomes extremely frustrating. Work is a blessing to mankind.

On many tombstones are engraved the words "At Rest,"

taken from the scripture, "Blessed are the dead which die in the Lord from henceforth: Yea, saith the Spirit, that they may rest from their labors, and their works do follow them" (Rev. 14:13).

Life often becomes burdensome, laden with sickness, financial struggles, sorrows. Problems arise which are personal, national and international and bring great stress into the lives of even Christians.

From all this we will be glad to rest. That does not mean, however, that we will spend eternity in idleness, for Revelation 22:3 assures us that "His servants shall serve him." And in Revelation 7:15 we read, concerning those who came out of great tribulation, "Therefore are they before the throne of God and serve him day and night in his temple. . . .

What will we be doing there? How will we be occupied? That is a vitally important question; in fact, the way we answer it is what life on earth is all about.

The parable of the talents compares the kingdom of heaven to a man going on a trip, who allotted money to his servants for their use during his absence. One received five talents, the other two, the third one. The first two servants put their talents to work, the third buried it. When the master returned he commended the two and promised that he would make them ruler over many things (Matt. 25:14-30).

The parable of the pounds (Luke 19:12-27) is similar, each servant receiving one pound. The servant who gained ten was commended and promised authority over ten cities. The other servant was likewise commended for gaining five pounds and was promised rulership over five cities.

Since these are called parables of the kingdom, the implication seems quite clear: faithful and industrious servants will be rewarded with positions and authority in the next world, according to how well each had fulfilled his individual potential.

God has foreordained the works that we should do (Eph. 2:10) and surely that plan includes far more than what we will be doing during our brief sojourn on earth. God has over us eternal purposes and plans regarding the future kingdom.

That God needs us for specific jobs in heaven may be illustrated by two incidents.

A man past middle age whom I knew as a minister became very ill. It was revealed to a saintly woman: "Don't try to keep him here by your prayers. He will be of more use to God in heaven at this time."

Live, a Sunday school paper, carried the story of Marian Carter. Just before her husband died, the Lord said to her, "I have need of him in heaven" (Springfield, Missouri: Gospel Publishing House, June 29, 1975).

These instances seem to indicate that just as an employer fits the person to the job, so does God have the same intention over His faithful children.

The scripture which tells us that we will be serving in heaven is confirmed by visions.

Robert Young (not the actor) tells of the experiences of a woman in which she described celestial spirits as being "variously employed; and although she felt inadequate to convey any definite idea of the nature of that employment, yet it appeared to be adapted to their mental tastes and spiritual attainments" (Lindsay, *True Visions*, pp. 38,39).

When Carol Hooley was taken to heaven, she asked the Lord about her father who was already there. Jesus told her that "he was happily active in the work of the Lord" (*Caught Up*, pp. 8-9).

Neither the scriptures nor visions give details as to the kind of activity there will be in heaven; so we'll have to wait until we get there to find out.

Improved Faculties and Capacities

A number of those who died and were revived said that

while in their spirit form they could see, hear and understand far better than before. We are told in 1 Corinthians 13:12 "For now we see through a glass darkly; but then face to face: now I know in part, but then shall I know even as also I am known." Some scientists say we are using only a very small part of our mental potential. Perhaps the Lord has so created man that the rest of his mental capacities will be used in heaven.

In his book, Sadhu Singh writes "there their goodness [referring to the righteous] is evident to all and it ever increases more and more, for nothing is present that can hinder their growth and everything that can sustain them is there to help them" (*Visions*, p. 29).

While he was in heaven Bunyan was informed by an inhabitant: "Here we have our capacities enlarged, according to the greatness of the objects we have to contemplate. While we were in the world below, no light could shine into our minds but through the windows of our senses, and therefore it was that the blessed God was pleased to condescend to our capacities and to adapt the expression of His majesty to the narrowness of our imaginations.

"But here the revelation of the Deity is much more glorious and our minds are clarified from all those earthly images that flow through the gross channels of the senses. Below, our purest conceptions of God were very imperfect. But here the gold is separated from the dross and our conceptions are more proper and becoming the simplicity and purity of God. Below the objects of glory were humbled to the perceptions of sense, but here the sensible faculties are raised and refined and made the subject of glory" (*Visions*, pp. 24,25).

We Shall Be Changed. What Does That Mean?

Many Christians have a misconception about the change

which takes place—either upon death or when Jesus comes. This error comes chiefly from a wrong interpretation of the scripture, "Beloved, now are we the sons of God, and it doth not yet appear what we shall be: but we know that when he shall appear, we shall be like him: for we shall see him as he is" (1 John 3:2).

The only important consideration, say some Christians, is that they be saved, because upon death they will suddenly be transformed from whatever kind of person they happened to be into a first-rate saint. They have the idea that in heaven everyone will be the same, like so many peas in a can.

This erroneous concept has lulled thousands of careless Christians into spiritual slumber and if they continue in their error, they may have a rude awakening during their first moments in heaven.

If it is true that when we see Jesus, or when we die in the Lord, that we shall immediately be changed to become like Him in character, then why does the following verse (1 John 3:3) say "and every man that hath this hope purifieth himself, even as he is pure?"

If we will all suddenly become as holy as Jesus, then why would we need to purify ourselves?

The change spoken of in this passage is clearly explained in two places:

For our conversation [citizenship] is in heaven; from whence also we look for the Saviour, the Lord Jesus Christ: Who shall *change our vile body*, that it may be fashioned like unto his glorious body, according to the working whereby he is able to subdue all things unto himself. (Phil. 3:20-21, italics mine)

Behold I show you a mystery; we shall not all sleep but we shall all be changed; In a moment, in the twinkling of an eye, at the last trump: for the trumpet shall sound and the dead shall be raised incorruptible and we shall be changed; *For this corruptible must put on incorruption and this mortal must put on immortality.* (1 Cor. 15:51-53, italics mine)

For those who are still living when Christ comes, the same change will take place, the change from corruption to incorruption.

These two scriptures show plainly that we shall become like Jesus physically, not spiritually.

The scriptures does speak of the saints being made perfect, but this refers to sin, for sin will have no place in heaven. Just before we enter that holy place, we will be perfected, in the sense of being cleansed from any remaining sin.

But this has nothing to do with spiritual maturity. Growth in the likeness of Jesus is a lifetime process, to which Christians ought diligently apply themselves in the power of the Holy Spirit. For it will make a vast difference regarding the kind of service for which souls will be fitted in eternity.

Miss Davis was given this truth. "The departure of the spirit from its unsettled and shattered habitation below worketh no change in its nature" (*Scenes*, p. 19).

Or, as Catherine Marshall put it, moments after death we will still be the same person we were while in the body (*To Live Again*, p. 24).

The kind of service with which we will be occupied in heaven will be that for which we made preparation while on earth. This does not mean that if we were accountants on earth, we will also be in heaven. But it does mean that if we have been "spiritual dropouts" while on earth, we will have to settle for the kinds of jobs in heaven for which we have qualified ourselves.

CHAPTER 10

Communion of
the Saints

Christians have always wondered whether the citizens of heaven are aware of what is happening on earth. The scripture hints that they do. "Wherefore, seeing we also are compassed about with so great a cloud of witnesses, let us lay aside every weight . . ." (Heb. 12:1). That cloud of witnesses refers to the saints of the Old Testament whose good records are described in the verses immediately preceding the one just quoted. Among them were Abel, Enoch, Noah and many others. It is these saints and those who have joined them subsequently who are looking upon earth. This does not mean that the saints in heaven are omniscient or omnipresent. However, at various times some are permitted to know some things.

Mr. Booth says that one saint in heaven told him, "Knowledge of the transactions of earth, for our sakes is very limited, but now and then we are permitted to get a glance of what is passing there" (*Visions*, p. 22).

The fact that dying people are often met by relatives and friends indicates that they must have received prior information about the coming of that one. However, because not everybody cares to so interpret this passage, we will drop the subject, only to pick up another one which is still more controversial.

Communion of the Saints

Are the saints in heaven allowed at times to minister to or be with those on earth? Also, are earth people ever allowed to enter heaven, in the spirit, to communicate with saints up there?

We are certainly not speaking here of spiritualism or anything which at all savors of the psychic or the occult. Nevertheless, false experiences should not be allowed to deprive us of true ones, originating in God. The most common creed of all Christendom, the Apostles' Creed, contains the phrase "I believe in the communion of the saints." This belief is based on the scripture mentioned above, concerning the cloud of witnesses. In her book *To Live Again* Catherine Marshall devotes a good part of her chapter 11 to this subject, in a decidedly affirmative way.

Sundar Singh, from whose book I often quote, has this to say about communication: "Some may consider these visions [referring to his book *Visions of Sadhu Sundar Singh of India*] are merely a form of spiritualism, but I would emphasize that there is one very essential difference. Spiritualism does presume to produce messages and signs from spirits out of the dark, but they are usually so fragmentary and unintelligible, if not actually deceptive, that they lead their followers away from rather than to the truth.

"In these visions on the other hand, I see vividly and clearly every detail of the glory of the spiritual world and I have the uplifting experience of very real fellowship with the saints, amid the inconceivably bright and beautiful world made visible. It is from these angels and saints that I have received, not vague, broken and illusive messages from the unseen, but clear and rational elucidations of many of the problems that have troubled me. . . .

"Once, in a vision, I asked the saints for a proof from the Bible of this communion of saints and was told it was to be found clearly given in Zechariah 3:7-8 where 'those that were standing by' were not angels but saints in glory; and God's promise on condition of Joshua fulfilling His command is that he will be given 'a place of access to walk among them (saints) that stand by,' and these are his 'fellows' the spirits of men made perfect with whom he could commune" (pp. 5-6).

Part of the above text follows: "Thus saith the Lord of hosts, If thou wilt walk in my ways and if thou wilt keep my charge, then thou shalt also judge my house and shalt also keep my courts, and I will give thee places to walk among those that stand by" (Zech. 3:7).

Many of the experiences recorded in this book strengthen the concept that communion with the saints does take place.

Sadhu Singh says that he received this information during one of his visits to heaven: "Our relatives and dear ones, and at times the saints as well, often come from the unseen world to help and protect us, but the angels always do. Yet they have never been allowed to make themselves visible to us, except at a few times of very special need.

"By ways unrecognized by us they influence us toward holy thoughts and incline us towards God and towards good conduct; and God's spirit dwelling in our hearts, completes that work for the perfecting of our spiritual life which they have been unable to accomplish" (*Visions*, p. 14).

While Miss Davis was visiting heaven, a spirit being said to her "This is the world [heaven] we know. Earth we visit, conducted by our guardian angels, but it is unlike Heaven. There we witness sorrow, pain and death; here harmony, happiness and life abide" (*Scenes*, p. 33).

During her last days Daisy Dryden, whose experience will be fully discussed in the chapter on children, was frequently visited by her predeceased brother, Allie. One time she said to her mother, "Mama, when I go away the Comforter will come to you and maybe He will let me come too sometimes; I'll ask Allie about it."

Mrs. Dryden said that Allie "seemed to be with her a great deal of the time during those last three days because when we asked her questions which she could not answer, she would say, 'Wait until Allie comes and I will ask him.' On this occasion she waited only a short time and then said, 'Allie says I may go to you sometimes; he says it is possible, but you will not know when I am there; but I can speak to your thought' (*Visions*, pp. 16-17).

In the booklet *Life after Death* (New York: Guideposts, n.d.) is an article ("The Blessed Assurance") written by Dr. Norman Vincent Peale in which he tells "when I was preaching at a Methodist gathering in Georgia, I had the most startling experience of all. At the end of the final session, the presiding Bishop asked all the ministers in the audience to come forward, form a choir and sing an old, familiar hymn.

"I was sitting on the speakers' platform, watching them come down the aisles. And suddenly, among them I saw my father. I saw him as plainly as I ever saw him when he was alive. He seemed about forty, vital and handsome. He was singing with the others.

"When he smiled at me and put up his hand in the old familiar gesture, for several unforgettable seconds it was as if my father and I were alone in that big auditorium. Then he was gone, but in my heart the certainty of his presence was indisputable. He was *there*, and I know that some day, somewhere, I'll meet him again" (pp. 3-4).

I personally had a brief visit from a person who had

recently died. Though it happened years ago, whenever I relate the incident, the presence of the Lord so greatly overshadows me and the listeners that I consider it another witness of the Spirit to its factualness.

Late at night, I was driving from a funeral of a friend in another city, alone on a major highway. Near the airport, traffic was so congested that I almost panicked. At that moment I distinctly felt the powerful presence of my deceased friend. For five minutes the car was filled with such an intense feeling of heavenly, almost overpowering love, that I can hardly describe it. I can only say that it must be the same kind of love which was felt by a number of others who had heavenly experiences. The very definite presence soon left, but there remained an afterglow of the atmosphere of heaven.

In November, 1975, I spoke to an old friend who wishes to be anonymous, whose husband had died a few years before. She told me that when her older sister died, she appeared to her, sat at the table and conversed with her. The deceased woman said she was all right and she was happy with the Lord.

When my friend told this story to her niece, daughter of the deceased woman, the niece cried excitedly, "Why, that's just what happened to me! Mother came to me and said everything was all right with her."

This same friend told me that when her husband died, three years before, he came to her several times. Once she was in a meeting where someone was playing an accordion. Because her husband had enjoyed accordion music very much, my friend said she wished her husband were present. Moments later she was astonished to see him walking down the aisle!

She said these visits occurred close to her husband's death, gradually diminished, then ceased altogether with the passage of time.

I am confident that many who are reading this book have had similar experiences. My personal conviction and that of many others is, "I believe in the communion of the saints."

CHAPTER 11

They Shall See His Face

Jesus said He was going away to prepare a place for us in the house of His Father (John 14:2). Since He himself would be the "architect and builder," it would be a place more beautiful than eye had ever seen or ear heard or heart had imagined (Heb. 11:10, TAB, 1 Cor. 2:9). Paradise, lovely as the garden of Eden and the New Jerusalem, sparkling with topaz, sapphire and emerald, would be an environment suitable for the eternal home of the bride of the King.

But what bride is content to live in a place when her Bridegroom is not there? However glorious the dwelling place, heaven would not be heaven without Him; for Christ himself is the chief attraction.

The deepest and holiest of all human emotions is awakened when a repentant sinner comes to Jesus and feels toward Him the surge of "love divine, all loves excelling." It is this devotion to the person of Christ which ever after motivates those who follow the Lamb withersoever He goeth.

For Him the fishermen gladly forsook their nets to become fishers of men. For His sake Paul left the company of men of culture to preach to barbarians the unsearchable riches of Christ. Mary broke her precious box of ointment to anoint the feet of her Beloved. And John, though exiled, still leaned on the bosom of Jesus.

Through the early years of the church there marched "a noble army, men and boys, the matron and the maid," who for the love of Jesus "climbed the steep ascent of Heaven through peril, toil and pain" (from the hymn, "The Son of God Goes Forth to War" by Reginald Heber). Their records, engraved in blood and tears are found in the eleventh chapter of Hebrews.

Down through the centuries Christians have chosen to be burned at the stake rather than deny Christ. Missionaries have followed His will into vermin-infested huts under a blazing tropical sun or crawled into frozen igloos to ignite hearts with the same love which burned in their own.

That is why Christians, having believed and followed Jesus, though they have never seen Him, will, upon arriving in heaven, ask only one question: "Where is Jesus? I want to see Him."

Speaking of the day when we are at last present with the Lord, the Psalmist exults, "As for me, I will behold thy face in righteousness: I shall be satisfied, when I awake, with thy likeness" (Ps. 17:15).

His likeness. What is this "likeness" to which the Psalmist refers? The scripture, "And they shall see his face" (Rev. 22:4), has been the theme of many old gospel songs: "Face to Face Shall I Behold Him," and "I Shall See Him Face to Face."

When that day comes for each of us and we look upon Him, what will be the appearance of this God-man in whom dwells all the fullness of the Godhead bodily and who is the "brightness of His glory and the express image of His person" (Heb. 1:3)?

We can find the answer in two ways: by descriptions of

those who saw God in scripture and by those who in our day saw Him in vision.

Even for scholars it is not always easy to be certain as to whether people in the Old Testament saw a vision of God the Father or God the Son. The distinction between the persons of Jesus and the Father and yet their unity will remain a mystery to be revealed only when we reach heaven. We have assumed that the Old Testament visions were always of God the Father, but this is not necessarily the case.

When Moses was on Mt. Sinai receiving the law and covenant he apparently saw God the Father in manifestations of fire, dark clouds, and the shaking of the mount (Deut. 4:11-12). In Isaiah's vision of God in the temple, he saw Him high and lifted up, His train filling the temple (Isa. 6:1-4). Ezekiel and Daniel also had awesome visions of the power and majesty of God (Ezek. 8:2-3; Dan. 7:9-10).

In his vision, John Bunyan saw "Deity exalted on the high throne of His glory, receiving the adoration of myriads of angels and saints, singing forth eternal hallelujahs and praises to Him, . . . too bright an object for mortality to view. Well may He therefore be called 'The God of Glory' for by His glorious presence He makes heaven what it is; there being rivers of pleasures perpetually springing from the divine Presence and radiating cheerfulness, joy and splendor to all the blessed inhabitants of heaven, the place of His happy residence and seat of His eternal empire" (*Visions*, pp. 15-16).

Since scripture says that no man can see God (the Father) and live (Exod. 33:20), some commentators believe that a number of the Old Testament visions were of Christ in a form foreshadowing His incarnation. This view seems to be confirmed by the fact that many of these Old Testament visions have in them elements which compare with the vision of Christ as seen by John in the Revelation.

New Testament visions of Christ were also majestic and awesome. On the Mount of Transfiguration the three disciples looked upon a glorified Jesus whose face shone as the sun and whose garments glistened with white light (Matt. 17:1-9). As did the Old Testament saints, they also fell on their faces with fear.

When Paul the Apostle saw the resurrected Christ, it was as though he looked directly into the brightness of the noonday sun. Blinded by the gaze of glory, he fell to the earth (Acts 26:13-15).

The description of Jesus as seen by John, recorded in the first chapter of the Revelation, corresponds in many ways to that of Daniel and Ezekiel. In John's vision, Jesus wore a long white garment with a golden girdle; His hair was white as wool, His eyes like a flame of fire, His feet as if they burned in a furnace and His voice as the sound of many waters. When John saw Him thus portrayed, he fell at His feet as dead.

As the first chapter of Revelation records John's vision of Christ, so the fourth chapter gives us a view of God. ". . . and, behold, a throne was set in heaven, and one sat on the throne. And he that sat was to look upon like a jasper [green] and a sardine [sardius, red] stone: and there was a rainbow round about the throne, in sight like unto an emerald. . . . And out of the throne proceeded lightnings and thunderings and voices . . ." (vv. 2,3,5). These descriptions would tend to make us understand how Moses felt at Mt. Sinai when so terrible was the sight that he said "I exceedingly fear and quake" (Heb. 12:21).

There was a reason why the Old Testament saints and those in the New Testament, who, when they saw God, became so frightened. Apparently God allowed them to see a measure of His power and glory which they were unable to bear. Even Daniel, after a vision "fainted, and was sick certain days" (Dan 8:27). If these holy men could hardly look upon the tremendous glory, how would it affect those of lesser spiritual stature?

It seems that for those newly arriving in heaven, the Lord must temper His glory to accommodate the limitations of their capacities.

While in vision, Singh learned that Christ reveals himself to the newly arrived in a dim way ". . . because at this stage they could not have endured a full exhibition of His glory. . . . When He does reveal Himself to anyone, He takes into account the particular stage of progress to which that soul has attained . . ." (*Visions*, p. 15).

But even this dimmed view was superlatively wonderful to each soul, says Singh. ". . . When these spirits saw Christ in this dim but attractive light, they were filled with a joy and peace which is beyond our power to describe. [They were] bathed in the rays of His lifegiving light and with the waves of His love which constantly flow out from Him . . ." (p. 16).

When Miss Davis saw Jesus she said "His loveliness can never be expressed. . . . Awed by His goodness, tenderness and love, I bowed . . . feeling that if worthy, I would worship Him" (*Visions*, p. 24).

Why is it that everyone who ever saw Jesus in vision felt the same way about Him? What is there about Him that draws such a response of love? John, called the Beloved and the Apostle of Love, explains in his epistle, "Herein is love, not that we loved God, but that he loved us . . ." (1 John 4:10). It is the love of God in Christ Jesus that first attracts us while we are still on earth, and in heaven it will be the same love which will draw us.

Many of those who had experiences of the next world said they became almost immediately aware of the most intense and wonderful love, so deep and penetrating that they felt immersed in an ocean of divine love.

This is what heaven is. "Where Jesus is, 'tis heaven there," says an old song. And where Jesus is, there is love; for God is love. It is the very essence of His being and personality.

Sadhu Singh was told by a celestial being "God who is love is seen in the person of Jesus sitting on the throne of the highest heaven. From Him who is the sun of righteousness and the light of the world, healing and life-giving rays and waves of light and love are seen flowing out through every saint and angel, bringing to whatever they touch vitalizing and vivifying power" (*Visions*, p. 29).

When asked if saints and angels who live in the highest spheres of heaven always look on the face of God and if they see Him, in what form and state does He appear, one of the saints replied "As the sea is full of water, so is the whole universe filled with God and every inhabitant of heaven feels His presence on every side" (p. 30).

Whether this presence or appearance is of Jesus or of the Father is not always clear, but because Jesus was made like unto His brethren, we would be inclined to think that we would feel more at home with Him.

If we should feel a little afraid of God the Father because of our concepts of Him through the Old Testament visions, it would be well to remember that these awesome sights were a display of only a part of His Being. God is not only the Great Eternal One, dwelling in a light which no man can approach, He is also the "Our Father which art in heaven," longsuffering, tender, compassionate, full of goodness and mercy, pitying His children as a father on earth.

But whether it be God the Father or God the Son or God the Holy Spirit, it will be our great glory and delight to be in the presence of God forever.

They Shall See His Face

When Jesus told His disciples that He was going to prepare a place for them in the house of His Father, He promised much more than a wonderful home for them. He said that He would come again to receive them *unto Himself*, "that where I am, there ye may be also" (John 14:3). So much does He love His bride that He wants her to be ever at His side.

This is what constitutes heaven—the Presence of God, which is the Presence of Love.

In that wonderful day when we at last see Jesus, we will burst forth into a paean of praise as expressed by one of His lovers of the 18th century:

O could I speak the matchless worth,
O could I sound the glories forth
Which in my Savior shine!

I'd sing the character He bears
And all the forms of love He wears,
Exalted on His throne,
In loftiest songs of sweetest praise,
I would to everlasting days
Make all His glories known.

Well, the delightful day will come
When my dear Lord will bring me home
And I shall see His face.
Then with my Savior, brother, friend,
A blest eternity I'll spend,
Triumphant in His grace.

Rev. Samuel Medley, 1789

CHAPTER 12

Hell—God's Provision of Mercy

They tortured the early Christians, burned them at the stake, threw them to the lions. Century upon century they raped, pillaged, destroyed. Under the trees of the Katyn Forest, they buried in mass graves 10,000 murdered Poles (Winston Churchill, *The Hinge of Fate* [Boston: Houghton, Mifflin Co., 1950] pp. 759-760), and slaughtered six million Jews in a planned program of starvation, forced labor and poison gas (Arthur D. Morse, *While Six Million Died*, [New York: Random House, 1967], p. 6,17,384).

Today they rob the aged, mutilate children, sell drugs to youth, get rich on pornography. In dimly lit halls Satanists offer human sacrifices and blaspheme the Son of God.

These are the *wicked*, of whom the scripture says "The wicked shall be turned into hell, and all the nations that forget God" (Ps. 9:17). No one denies that sinners such as these have earned severe punishment. But what disturbs many is this question: How can a God of love send *ordinary* sinners to hell? People like your atheist neighbor, who will travel miles out of his way to help an old man in need. Philanthropists whose millions build hospitals for the poor. Doctors, professors, scientists dedicated to serve mankind, yet who call the Bible folklore and God a myth.

Whatever may be our personal feelings or reasonings about that question, we can look only to scripture for the answer. In the last book of the Bible is a verse linking the "ordinary sinner," if you want to so identify him, with the truly wicked.

But the fearful, and *unbelieving*, and the abominable, and murderers, and whoremongers, and sorcerers, and idolaters, and all liars, shall have their part in the lake which burneth with fire and brimstone: which is the second death. (Rev. 21:8, italics mine)

The Fact of Hell

The Bible acknowledges only two places: heaven and hell. The most convincing proof of the existence of hell are the words of Jesus himself, who is the supreme authority.

. . . whosoever shall say to his brother . . . Thou fool, shall be in danger of hell fire. (Matt. 5:22)
And shall cast them into a furnace of fire; there shall be wailing and gnashing of teeth. (Matt. 13:42)
Ye serpents, ye generation of vipers, how can ye escape the damnation of hell? (Matt. 23:33)
And these shall go away into everlasting punishment: but the righteous into life eternal. (Matt. 25:46)

These and other scriptures can neither be ignored nor rationalized away. The message of hell is as plain as that concerning heaven.

Testimony of Visions

To corroborate scripture, God has chosen certain of His followers to whom He has entrusted visions of both heaven and hell. In their books, Bunyan, Miss Davis, Singh and others supply many details concerning life in hell. In addition, we have scores of records of the reactions of individual sinners at the moment of death.

Some of these unfortunate persons stared in horror at objects visible only to them; others screamed "I am in the flames," or "Pull me out, they're dragging me down!"

It is commonly known that despite a written retraction, atheist Voltaire spent his last few months in remorse and fear of hell so horrible that his nurse said never again would she attend a dying atheist.

The Bible says "And whosoever was not found written in the book of life was cast into the lake of fire" (Rev. 20:15). Would that include Voltaire, Paine, Nero, Hitler? What about liberal theologians and professors who destroyed the faith of thousands of young students? Or the factory laborer who with curses and blasphemies sneers "There is no heaven or hell. When I die, I will be fertilizer." Or the mother who never attended church and brought up her children without the knowledge of God?

What Happens at Death?

What happens to all sinners, the great ones as well as the ordinary, when they close their mortal eyes and open their spiritual eyes, to discover that they are still very much alive?

Very simply Jesus tells us, in the story of Lazarus and the rich man. ". . . The beggar died and was carried by the angels into Abraham's bosom; the rich man also died and was buried. And in hell he lifted up his eyes, being in torments . . ." (Luke 16:22-23). Since the righteous man was carried into heaven by the angels, we could infer that the spirit of the wicked man must have been taken into hell by evil spirits.

This view is supported by visions of those who saw into hell. Singh said that many sinners at death "see hideous and devilish faces of the evil spirits that have come around them and become speechless and paralyzed by fear." In one instance he saw that "the evil spirits almost immediately led these souls away toward the darkness. For when [they were] in the flesh, they had consistently allowed evil spirits to influence them for evil and had willingly permitted themselves to be enticed to all kinds of wickedness" (*Visions*, pp. 9,11).

During her vision, recorded in *Scenes Beyond the Grave*, Marietta Davis saw that "Over the battlefields were congregated spirits of the dead and according to the moral nature of the dying, there were attending spirits who awaited their arrival in the spirit world. . . . This intermediate state or vestibule of the spirit world is visited by beings varying in character from the unholy and wretched to the bright and sanctified angels who in multitudes congregate at the portals of death, as messengers of God" (p. 20).

So we understand that accompanied by evil spirits, the souls of the unrighteous are taken into hell.

Different Planes

At this point someone will ask, Do all the unconverted—the extremely wicked as well as the common sinner—go to the same part of hell?

In most modern jails some attempt is made to separate the novice criminal from the hardened one. After trial, the judgment of the murderer is much more severe than that of the petty thief. One scripture seems to indicate that it may be similar in the next world.

And that servant, which knew his lord's will, and prepared not himself, neither did according to his will, shall be beaten with many stripes. But he that knew not, and did commit things worthy of stripes, shall be beaten with few stripes. For unto whomsoever much is given, of him shall be much required: and to whom men have committed much, of him they will ask the more. (Luke 12:47-48)

Visions indicate that as each saint is assigned a place in heaven compatible with his spiritual stature, so the wicked also are punished in proportion to their sins.

This is corroborated further by Singh who learned through a vision: "In the dark part of the world which is called hell, there are many grades and planes. The particular one in which any spirit lives in suffering is dependent on the quantity and character of his sins" (*Visions*, p. 24).

Kind of Punishment

Scripture makes it very plain that hell will be a place of fire and brimstone, of weeping and wailing and gnashing of teeth. We are not informed concerning the exact nature of the suffering, or whether it will be physical or mental or both. It is interesting to read the description of Miss Davis's visit to hell, in which one person related the following:

"This realm, curtained with a cloud of nether night is one sea of perverted and diseased magnetic element. Here lust, pride, hate, avarice, love of self, ambition, contention and blasphemies, [and] reveling in madness, kindle into a burning flame.

"And that specialty of evil which does not belong to and enfold one spirit, belongs to and enfolds from another, so that the combined strength of the aggregate of all is the prevailing law. By this strength of evil I am bound and in it I exist" (*Scenes*, p. 66).

Many more details concerning the kind of suffering endured are described by Bunyan, Davis and Singh. They could be classified roughly into four divisions:

1. Much of the sorrow will be self-inflicted by remorse over lost opportunities, regret over sins and past doubts concerning the existence of heaven and hell.

2. Great suffering will also be occasioned by association with other unregenerate souls. In heaven there will be continual interchange of love; here it will be hate, revilings, scorn, recriminations.

3. Great pain will be inflicted by Satan himself, king of that underground universe of torment. There for the first time, those who had on earth allowed themselves to be deceived by the Father of Lies will see him as he is, stripped of his disguise as an "angel of light." In his true nature as the enemy of their souls, Satan's greatest joy will be to increase their misery.

4. The worst suffering will be that of separation from God and all that He embodies.

Moral Nature Unchanged

We must remember that upon death the moral nature of the sinner remains unchanged. The scripture says "He that is unjust, let him be unjust still; and he which is filthy, let him be filthy still . . ." (Rev. 22:11). If while in the body a man hated God, cursed, blasphemed, committed murder and adultery, denied God's existence, was contentious, jealous, proud, cruel, then in his spirit form he will remain the same. Would we want such in heaven? Were they present, they would soon pollute and make a hell of paradise.

Regarding our earthly associations we are told "Be ye not unequally yoked together with unbelievers; for what fellowship hath righteousness with unrighteousness? and what communion hath light with darkness? And what concord hath Christ with Belial? or what part hath he that believeth with an infidel?" (2 Cor. 6:14-15). How much more would that be true of trying to unite the Kingdom of

94

Darkness with the Kingdom of Light!

As the two classes on earth are separated by an invisible barrier, so will they be in the next world. "And beside all this, between us and you there is a great gulf fixed: so that they which would pass from hence to you cannot; neither can they pass to us that would come from thence" (Luke 16:26).

Sinners Would Be Happier in Hell

The truth is that the sinner could not bear the atmosphere of heaven. This is shown by a vision of Sundar Singh. Once while he was in the other world, he saw a wicked man cursing and reviling God. "One of the high angels said to him, 'God gives permission that this man may be brought into heaven.' Eagerly this man stepped forward, accompanied by two angels; but when they reached the door of heaven and he saw the holy and light-enveloped place and the glorious and blessed inhabitants that dwell there, he began to feel uneasy. The angels said to him, 'See how beautiful a world is this! Go a little farther and look at the Lord sitting on His throne.'

"From the door this man looked and then as the light of the Sun of righteousness revealed to him the impurity of his sin-defiled life, he started back in agony of self-loathing and fled with such precipitance that he did not even stop in the intermediate state of the world of spirits, but like a stone he passed through it and cast himself headlong into the bottomless pit" (*Visions*, p. 19).

Miss Davis was given the same insight, that sinners would be "happier" in hell. At a later period in her visit to hell and while she herself was allowed to experience the feeling of a lost soul, Miss Davis said she longed to go to heaven. "But little did I know that even then, were I permitted to enter . . . that I should suffer excess of agony from the effects of the love and harmony of heaven upon me; so that my condition would involve me in perplexity and misery equal to the deepest hell" (*Scenes*, p. 89).

Hell Is a Provision of God's Wisdom and Mercy

Also to Miss Davis was given the further understanding that because sinners would be miserable in heaven, that hell is actually a provision of God's wisdom and mercy.

Her angel guide told her about "the wisdom of a benevolent Creator in the bestowment of that Providence which causes spirits of like nature and tendencies, whose habits are established, to incline to like conditions and abodes, so that opposite elements of absolute good and evil, being separate, shall not enhance the misery or annoy the bliss of other classes. . . . Herein is displayed the wisdom and goodness of God. No absolutely discordant element in the world of spirits mingles with the pure and hamonious" (*Scenes*, p. 90-91).

And there shall in no wise enter into it any thing that defileth, neither whatsoever worketh abomination, or maketh a lie: but they which are written in the Lamb's book of life. (Rev. 21:27)

This explains that when God allows the sinful to go to hell, He really is being merciful, for the sinner would be more miserable in heaven than in hell.

God Never Planned Hell

God never planned that there should be a hell. The Bible opens with "In the beginning God created the heavens and the earth." Nothing is said about hell because there was no need for it. But when Satan fell and drew with him one-third of the angels, God then created a place appropriate for him. Scripture says hell was "prepared for the devil and his angels" (Matt. 25:41).

Tragically, not only did Satan win a following in heaven among the angels who joined in his rebellion against God, but since that time, Satan began to draw to himself a portion of humanity. Thousands upon thousands of the sons of darkness have already died and their spirits have gone into the dark world.

Just as the righteous remain in paradise, awaiting the time of the resurrection when their bodies and spirits shall be united again, so now all the followers of Satan are in a section of hell, awaiting the resurrection of the wicked dead. At the end of time a great drama will take place, with three sets of actors:

1. The beast and the false prophet.
   "And the beast was taken, and with him the false prophet. . . . These both were cast alive into a lake of fire burning with brimstone." (Rev. 19:20)

2. Next, God will deal with Satan himself.
   "And the devil that deceived them was cast into the lake of fire and brimstone, where the beast and the false prophet are, and shall be tormented day and night forever and ever." (Rev. 20:10)

3. And finally, the followers of Satan.
   "And whosoever was not found written in the book of life was cast into the lake of fire." (Rev. 20:15)

When Bunyan visited hell, one of its inhabitants said to him, "In this sad dark abode of misery and sorrow we have lost the presence of the ever blessed God. And this is that which makes this dungeon hell. Though we had lost a thousand worlds, it would not be so much as this one loss.

Could but the least glimpse of His favor enter here, we might be happy; but we have lost it, to our everlasting woe" (*Visions*, p. 45).

The scripture says that "The fool hath said in his heart, There is no God" (Ps. 14:1).

He is a fool indeed who is willing to take the remotest chance of spending eternity in hell.

CHAPTER 13

The Shining Ones

Whoever it is that conducts the souls of the wicked to the Kingdom of Darkness—whether it be evil spirits, demons or fallen angels—most Christians believe that the spirits of the just are taken to the Kingdom of Light by angels.

Since so many books, tracts and articles have been written about these radiant creatures, one of the most recent being *Angels, God's Secret Agents* by Billy Graham, this chapter will cover only general information. The main emphasis here will be upon angels as they relate to heaven.

Who are the angels? What is their origin? What part do they play in the lives of earth people? What about guardian angels? Some of the answers given here will be familiar, others you may find surprising.

Origin and Purpose

How did angels come to be? All we know is that at some point in the distant and mysterious past, before the world and man were made, God created the angels as spirit beings. ". . . Who maketh his angels spirits and his ministers a flame of fire" (Heb. 1:7).

Why did God create the angels? The Psalmist tells us they

are to worship God and to do His will. "Bless the Lord, ye his angels, that excel in strength, that do his commandments, hearkening unto the voice of his word; Bless ye the Lord all ye his hosts, ye ministers of his, that do his pleasure" (Ps. 103:20-21).

The Ministry of Angels on Earth

Among the over 600 references to angels in the Bible are many acts of supernatural ministry. In the Old Testament they comforted Jacob, encouraged Joshua, instructed the parents of Samson, baked a cake for Elijah, closed the mouths of lions. The New Testament begins with an angelic appearance to Zechariah, later to Mary, then to the shepherds. They ministered to Jesus; an angel delivered Peter from prison, talked to Philip, Cornelius, Paul. Their ministries were as varied as the needs of those to whom God sent them.

In contemporary times perhaps the most frequent supernatural experiences have been associated with the ministry of angels. While she was in heaven, Marietta Davis said "above and around me and far in the distance were passing and repassing with the quickness of thought, spirits of pure light. 'These,' said my guide, 'are ministering angels; their supreme delight is to go upon errands of mercy. Their home is with the ever blest. They are employed as guardian protectors and messengers to those in conditions below them' " (*Scenes*, p. 21).

Besides such records as the above, some of which were written years ago, many Christians can relate a true angel story, either something he himself experienced or read in a book or tract. Since many of these are well-known, I will include only a few less familiar incidents.

In time of need, a saintly German woman, now deceased, with whom I was acquainted, was driven home by a stranger. When she got out of the car and turned to thank her benefactor, both car and driver had completely disappeared.

When a friend severely injured his wrist and prayed earnestly, he was visited by a seven-foot angel, who touched and instantly healed the wrist.

A truck driver completely lost control on an icy road. As his semitrailer jackknifed and headed into oncoming cars on the opposite lane, he took his hands off the wheel and asked God to take over. The truck was miraculously steered to safety, at which time the man placed his hands back on the wheel.

These are records of known instances of angelic intervention. But no one knows how many times each of us in our lifetime, without being aware of it, was helped by one of these invisible ministers of God.

Numbers

Angels are numbered in scripture from "twenty thousand, even thousands of angels," mentioned in the Psalms (68:17), to the "multitude of the heavenly host" seen by shepherds at the birth of Christ, as recorded in the Gospels (Luke 2:13) and further, there is the scene in Revelation where John ". . . beheld and . . . heard the voice of many angels . . . and the number of them was ten thousand times ten thousand, and thousands of thousands" (5:11).

After Bible days, recorded visions and experiences of many saints confirm the presence of angels. Though most individuals saw only one or a few, some, like John Bunyan, looked upon an "innumerable host of bright attendants who welcomed [him] into that blissful sea of happiness" (*Visions*, p. 29).

101

Rank

Among these heavenly hosts there seem to be diversities in rank, type and responsibility. Though angels seem to be most numerous, there are at least two archangels, plus cherubim, seraphim and the strange "four beasts" (living creatures) of Revelation (4:8). Some of them were seen by General Booth who wrote "Floating about me were beautiful beings whom I felt by instinct were angels and archangels, seraphim and cherubim" (*Visions*, p. 10).

During his visit to heaven, John Bunyan was informed that "even among God's flaming angels there are diversities of order and different degrees of glory" (*Visions*, p. 29).

Singh mentioned speaking to "an angel who had come from the highest grades of heaven and who occupied a high position there" (*Visions*, p. 32).

Appearance

Perhaps the first question a person asks of the one who has seen an angel is "What did he look like?"

From scripture and from more recent visions, we can obtain a relatively complete picture. The angels who were seen at the tomb of Jesus were described as two men "in shining garments" (Luke 24:4). The ascension of Jesus was accompanied by two men "in white apparel" (Acts 1:10). From this we might conclude that at least some of the angels looked like human beings.

Other angels appeared in more supernatural form, such as the angel described by Matthew, also at the tomb of Jesus: "His countenance was like lightening, and his raiment white as snow" (28:3).

The visions of those who saw into the next world also mentioned varied manifestations of angels. When Marietta Davis was taken to heaven, she said ". . . lo, in the distance and above me I saw a light descending, having the appearance of a brilliant star. As it advanced its halo illuminated the expanse about me . . . I began to discover the outlines of what appeared to me a glorified human being. Gradually the figure became more distinct, until poised in the atmosphere before and above me was an angel whose excellence far exceeded the highest concept . . . of my human thought. The form, more lovely than language has power to portray, silently moved as it drew near me" (*Scenes*, p. 16).

Unusually vivid descriptions of angels appear in *Vanya*, by Myrna Grant, the story of a Russian youth who was martyred by the Communists. Ivan Moiseyev writes that during his trial he had his second vision of an angel. "The sun shone brightly in the blue sky. Suddenly from heaven began to descend a bright star which was coming closer and becoming bigger. I saw it was an angel.

"He came down, not entirely to the ground, about 200 meters above and walked in the air above me in the same direction in which my road led. He said, 'Ivan, go, don't be afraid. I am with you.' He walked right up to the door of the headquarters, then he became invisible to me . . . I believe he was by my side inside the headquarters when I spoke with the superiors.

"About two months ago . . . I prayed all night. At three or four in the morning . . . God showed me the heavenly choir which sang 'In all the ends of this unhappy earth.' While the angels were singing this song, I saw them. They were all in many-colored, bright garments. When they disappeared the Lord said to me, 'This is for the comfort of your soul. Tomorrow you will leave from here.' And so it was" (*Vanya*, pp. 163,164).

The scriptures do not usually tell us whether or not the angels who commonly appeared to Bible characters had wings, but several references in Revelation speak of angels "flying through the midst of heaven" (8:13; 14:6). The beings in Isaiah 6:2 had six wings; those in Ezekiel had four and the carved cherubim on the Ark of God had two wings (Ezek. 1:5-6; Exod. 25:20).

Daisy Dryden said that when angels came to her they did not fly, but simply appeared (*Visions*, p. 22).

However, the ones General Booth saw did have wings. ". . . the sky was full of white-winged, happy, worshiping, joyous beings . . ." (*Visions*, p. 11).

Because descriptions are somewhat generalized, we might tend to think that all angels look alike, without any distinct personality or distinguishing features, like paper cut-outs or the cloudlike masses of angels seen in Sunday school pictures. Such preconceived ideas make it difficult for us to think of angels as being individuals and personal. Still, when we remember that God knows all the stars and ". . . calleth them all by their names" (Ps. 147:4), He must surely know each of His own angels by name and individual appearance and personality.

This view is given some weight by something which was told to Miss Davis while she was in heaven: ". . . No two edifices [in heaven] are perfectly alike in interior beauty, external form or decoration but all harmoniously combine, and also that each guardian angel is different in radiative light and individuality of the face and form. This you are permitted to know" (*Scenes*, p. 37).

Angels as Musicians

Throughout the Bible, instrumental and vocal music is mentioned as being a part of worship to God, both on earth and also in heaven. The four living creatures around the throne accompanied their singing with harps, somewhat as we do on earth with guitars (Rev. 5:8-9). The Weymouth version of this passage says that angels also sing. "And I looked, and heard the voices of many angels on every side of the throne, and of the living creatures and the Elders numbering myriads of myriads and thousands of thousands, and in loud voices they were singing, 'Worthy is the Lamb which has been slain . . .' " (Rev. 5:11-12).

Something of their joyous nature is revealed in a scripture in Job: "When the morning stars sang together, and all the sons of God shouted for joy" (38:7).

Since music is an integral part of life in the next world, we would expect those having visions to be aware of it. Mrs. Bossert said, "Then suddenly I began to hear strains of sweet heavenly music from the celestial land. It can never be compared with earthly music" (*My Visit*, p. 7).

Mrs. McKay related that as she was being taken to heaven "The singing and the music from the angels as we traveled upward is beyond my words to describe" (Lindsay, *True Visions*, p. 34).

During Miss Davis' extended visit to heaven, she often mentioned singing and instrumental music of angels. "The parts of music performed were manifold, yet in harmony; and the melody was the beauty of perfection" (*Scenes*, p. 92).

Guardian Angels

One of the most provocative thoughts in regard to this subject is whether or not each person actually has one or more guardian angels continually present with him.

Jesus' birth was announced by angels. They ministered to Him when He was tempted by the devil and in the garden of Gethsemane; they were present during His burial and resurrection. In His ascension He was attended by angels and will be when He returns to earth.

If our lives should parallel His, then we too would be attended by angels from birth to death. At least two scriptures seem to indicate this. "Take heed that ye despise not one of these little ones; for I say unto you, that in heaven their angels do always behold the face of my Father which is in heaven" (Matt. 18:10). When Peter came out of prison and stood at the gate, the disciples couldn't believe it was he. "And they said unto her [Rhoda] Thou art mad. But she constantly affirmed that it was even so. Then said they [mistakenly], It is his angel" (Acts 12:15). The use of these two words "their angel" and "his angel" seems to indicate a belief that each individual has one or more personal angels. The following scripture also seems relevant. "Are they not all ministering spirits, sent forth to minister for them who shall be heirs of salvation?" (Heb. 1:14).

It seems also that angels are constantly watching us for ". . . we are made a spectacle [margin, theater] unto the world, and to angels, and to men" (1 Cor. 4:9). Consider also this scripture: "The angel of the Lord encampeth round about them that fear him, and delivereth them" (Ps. 34:7).

If these are indeed our personal guardian spirits, then we are well taken care of.

In describing a scene in heaven, Miss Davis also spoke about guardians: "Mingling as permitted with the inhabitants of earth are countless guardian angels. No day nor hour nor moment passes, but each mortal is watched by the spirit appointed to his charge" (*Scenes*, p. 30).

Angels Escort Us to Heaven

The most delightful and triumphant ministry of an angel must be to convey to heaven the soul over whom he had charge from the day of his birth. It is a time of special joy because that soul has safely come "through many dangers, toils and snares."

The only scripture that refers to this special task seems to be the one found in the story of the rich man and Lazarus.

"And it came to pass, that the beggar died, and was carried by the angels into Abraham's bosom . . ." (Luke 16:22). Perhaps no other single scripture has been so fully corroborated by the experiences of those who had visions or who saw into the next world at the moment of death.

In his book of visions, Singh says that he was informed while there that "to conduct the souls of men from the world is the duty of angels" (*Visions*, p. 10).

In speaking of the death of a believer, Singh said "He [the Christian] is extremely happy for he sees angels and saintly spirits coming to welcome him. Then too, his loved ones who have died before are permitted to attend his deathbed and to conduct his soul to the spiritual world" (*Visions*, p. 10).

For a number of reasons, angels are needed to escort souls, the obvious one being that the person wouldn't know the location of heaven and would be unable to transport himself through space alone. Another reason, however, which was more fully covered in Chapter 7, Paradise, is that the soul must pass through the hostile territory of the Prince of the power of the air. But with a heavenly escort, the journey is safely made.

Ministry in Heaven

Although the Bible does not say so, it would seem reasonable to believe that since angels have always ministered to God and His people while they were on earth, they would continue to do so in heaven. Saints arriving in paradise in various levels of mental and spiritual development would surely need much help and instruction for further growth in their new and permanent home.

In a number of instances, Singh tells of various ones in heaven who received instruction from angels especially appointed to the work of preparing them for higher spheres of existence in the heavenly kingdom.

As angels have been an important though invisible part of man's life on earth, so after he arrives in heaven, angels will undoubtedly continue to be his now visible and delightful companions and helpers in heaven.

Worship

One of the most glorious ministries of angels in heaven is that of worship to God. We are told of God the Father ". . . when he bringeth in the firstbegotten into the world, he saith, And let all the angels of God worship him . . ." (Heb. 1:6).

The 103rd Psalm exhorts angels to "Bless the Lord" (v. 20-21), and the fourth chapter of Revelation described the work of the four "living creatures" who rest not day and night saying "Holy, holy, holy, Lord God Almighty; which was, and is, and is to come" (v. 8).

Like a mighty anthem, we hear again the worship of the heavenly beings: "Worthy is the Lamb that was slain to receive power, and riches, and wisdom, and strength, and honour, and glory, and blessing" (Rev. 5:11,12,14). Thus do the angels fulfill the purpose of their existence, to serve and worship and glorify God.

CHAPTER 14

"Little Ones to Him Belong"

One of the most distressing sights in a cemetery is a tombstone with a little lamb on it. Death is usually associated with advancing or old age, but in 1974 the Grim Reaper claimed 9,831 children between the ages of one and four and 14,636 between five and fourteen—a total of 24,467 youngsters (Vital Statistics of the U.S., Vol. 2, Part A, 1974, Table 1-26, U.S. Department of Health, Education and Welfare, Public Health Service, Rockville, Md. 20852).

But another "cemetery" is still more pathetic. Since the legalization of abortions, who knows how many thousands of fetuses were dropped into hospital garbage cans! The Right To Life Committee of Chicago estimates a conservative figure of at least one and a half million of such "burials" in 1975.

We will consider in this chapter the continuation of life in heaven of the souls of older children, as well as of those whose spirits departed from the merest beginnings of a physical form. The sources are the Bible and present day records of children who died and were buried, and of children who died and were revived.

The Bible records the death of a number of children, some

very young and some older. When the infant son of David and Bathsheba died, David said ". . . I shall go to him, but he shall not return to me" (2 Sam. 12:23). A much older child, perhaps teen-aged, the son of the wicked King Jeroboam, was permitted to die young lest he become contaminated with his father's evil ways. (See Chapter 5, The Appointed Time.)

The Bible also contains several records of children who died and were restored to life. One such account involves the dead child over whom Elijah prayed ". . . O Lord my God, I pray thee, let this child's soul come into him again. And the Lord heard the voice of Elijah and the soul of the child came into him again and he revived" (1 Kings 17:21-23).

Another account is in the New Testament; Jairus came to Jesus crying "My daughter is even now dead: but come and lay thy hand upon her and she shall live. . ." (Matt. 9:18-25). And Jesus "took her by the hand and the maid arose." She was twelve years old.

We are not told anything of the experiences of these two Bible children while their spirits were briefly in heaven. But we do have testimonies of modern day children who died, saw into heaven and were revived.

Among the hundreds of patients interviewed by Dr. Kubler-Ross were a number of children. She used the experiences of some of them as one of the proofs that those who saw into the next world were not hallucinating.

We quote from an article in the *Chicago Tribune* dated May 23, 1976: "Kubler-Ross notes that 'skeptical scientists say this is simply thought projection.' But she contends: 'It cannot be, because when I asked five- or six-year-olds who have had this experience whom they see, not one has seen Mommy or Daddy. It was always a dead person.' "

In the June 17, 1976 issue of the NATIONAL INQUIRER, Dr. Kubler-Ross related the following about a twelve-year-old girl who saw beyond. The girl told her father that she was met by her dead brother and that she experienced a great sense of love. She said she didn't want to return but was sent back. "It was wonderful," she said. . . . "But I don't have a dead brother, do I?" Weeping, her parents admitted she did but that they never told her about him.*

Children's Paradise

It seems that a special place in heaven is reserved for children. At the time Mrs. Julia Ruopp was out of her body she found herself looking into a bright spot of heaven. "What I saw there made all earthly joys pale into insignificance. I longed to join the merry throng of children, singing and frolicking in an apple orchard. . ." (*Window of Heaven*, p. 29).

Telling about the death of a young child, Singh said "Then the angels took the child's soul to that beautiful, light-filled part of heaven which is set apart for children, where they care for them and teach them in all heavenly wisdom, until gradually the little ones become like angels" (*Visions*, p. 12).

Do Children Grow Up in Heaven?

Many have wondered whether children continue to grow in heaven. Scripture is silent, but vision affirms what we instinctively feel to be true. In God there is no standing still. Because the Bible often speaks of spiritual growth from infancy to maturity, we would expect the same progress to be present in heaven.

Numbers said that they were greeted by predeceased children who though now being full grown, as well as free from former physical defects, were recognized.

Excerpt reprinted by permission of THE NATIONAL INQUIRER.

Premature Infants

Theologians and physicians differ as to when the fetus becomes a human being, some of those believing it to be not until several months use this concept to justify the practice of abortion.

In literature distributed by the Illinois Right To Life Committee are these statements: A New York court admitted "in the contemporary medical view, the child begins a separate life from the moment of conception. At conception a genetically unique individual begins life. All the characteristics he or she will have as an adult are already determined [in the genes and chromosomes] including eye color, skin pigmentation, sex and intelligence potential."

If we believe that a fetus is a person (though an undeveloped one), when he dies or is aborted, then he has a soul which is taken by the angels into heaven.

Miss Davis seems to have had a special revelation concerning what happens to these embryo spirits when they arrive in the world of light. During her vision, she saw an angel carrying a tiny "pale light" which she was told was an infant spirit. The angel said to her "that which is nourished by each angel is a spirit whose being is just begun and who by reason of nature's violated laws has been separated prematurely from its infant form in the external world. . . .

"The Quickening Spirit [of God] gives energy and expansion to the life principle unfolding so that the intellect may perceive, the judgment operate, the understanding embrace realities and the being enjoy the life thereof" (*Scenes*, p. 44).

Classification of Infants

An angel also informed Miss Davis "Whenever an infant dies on earth, the angel guardian who bears up the spirit to the Land of Peace perceives its interior type of mind and according to its type it is classed with others of like order and intelligence . . . and according to their variety of artistic, scientific and social tendencies assigns each a home best adapted to the unfolding of its interior germs of life into intellectual, artistic or industrial harmony" (*Scenes*, p. 37).

Instruction

Much of *Scenes Beyond the Grave* by Marietta Davis is devoted to the detailed instructions concerning the training which infants and children receive as they move into higher schools of learning and degrees of development.

All children of course need instruction in order to develop. But infants and very young children who die before the years of accountability need a special kind concerning redemption.

The last book of the Bible, from which we learn much about heaven, calls the Lord Jesus "The Lamb" twenty-one times. Therefore, we know that even in heaven the cross will be forever remembered.

The spirits of premature infants and very young children in heaven would have to understand why the saints and angels cry "Worthy is the Lamb that was slain. . ." (Rev. 5:12). Therefore, one of the most important preliminary tasks of angels will be to teach children redemption's story.

"Jesus Loves the Little Children"

In all of this preparation and development of infants the Lord takes a deep and loving interest. The biblical passages concerning children amply reveal the attitude of Jesus toward the little ones. "Let the little children come to me and do not hinder them. . ." (Matt. 19:14, WEYMOUTH). He held children on His lap, took infants into His arms, probably stroked their hair, smiled lovingly into their eyes, told them stories or played with them. Even on His human side, being the oldest in the family of His mother, he had enough contact with children to understand their ways and to love them.

In the account of her vision, Carol Hooley described a scene in which Jesus' love for an infant was displayed. Mrs. Hooley's daughter, Cinday, saw in a vision "a beautiful room in heaven where a baby was being presented to the Lord by an angel. She saw the Lord put this baby in a bed and even told us the color of the blanket. She then saw the angels caring for the many babies there" (*Caught up to Heaven* [Denver: Liberty Publications], p. 11).

Not long after they had prayed about what this should mean, the family received word that the tiny baby daughter of a loved one had died at the time of the vision.

The Story of Daisy Dryden

Among the more graphic descriptions of certain aspects of the next world were those given by ten-year-old Daisy Dryden before she died. The book was written by her mother in 1894.

Since the child's father was a Methodist Episcopal minister, Daisy received religious training, but she was in no wise unusual nor did she possess psychic powers. Neither could her experience be attributed to hallucinations because she was rational to the moment of death. Since she was three days in dying, she hovered between two worlds, being conscious of both during this time.

One afternoon toward the close of her illness, she joyfully informed her father that she had seen Jesus and that she was going to heaven to be with Him.

During her last three days she began to communicate with Allie, her brother who had died seven months before. "He seemed to be with her a great deal of the time," her mother wrote, "because when we asked her questions which she

114

could not answer, she would say 'Wait until Allie comes and I will ask him.' On this occasion she waited only a short time and then said 'Allie says I may go to you sometimes; he says it is possible, but you will not know when I am there, but I can speak to your thought.' "

When Daisy's parents asked how the next world looked she replied "I can't describe it. It is so different, I couldn't make you understand."

One day Daisy was visited by a neighbor, Mrs. B., who was in deep distress, having just lost her husband and twelve-year-old son. When she asked Daisy about them, she replied, "Bateman is here and says he is alive and well and is in such a good place, he would not come home for anything."

Mrs. B. asked Daisy to ask Bateman whether his father was there. Daisy replied, "He says he is not here and says to you, 'Mother, don't fret about me; it is better I did not grow up.' "

The same day, her Sunday school teacher, Mrs. H., asked Daisy about her two children who died some years ago.

When Daisy described them, the mother said "How can that be? They were children when they died." Daisy answered "Allie says 'Children do not stay children; they grow up as they do in this life.' " Mrs. H. then said, "but my little Mary fell and was so injured that she could not stand straight." To this Daisy replied, "She is all right now; she is straight and beautiful and your son is looking so noble and happy."

Another friend told about her daughter who also died some years ago, but the mother did not recognize her from Daisy's description. When Daisy said, "She used to have a mark of a mole on the left side of her neck, but she does not have it now," the mother was convinced.

Once Daisy said "Look mama, there is Mrs. E. standing at the foot of the bed." Her mother said, "I can't see her." "I know," replied Daisy, "no one unless he has dying eyes can see spirits, but she says to tell you, you were right, she is with the saved."

Once her mother asked how she saw the angels. Daisy replied, "I do not see them all the time. But when I do, the walls seem to go away and I can see ever so far and you could not begin to count the people. Some are near and I know them, others I have never seen before."

Another time she said, "Mama, I wish you could see Allie; he is standing beside you . . . He says you cannot see him because your spirit eyes are closed, but that I can because my body only holds my spirit . . . by a thread of life."

Her mother asked further, "Daisy, how does Allie appear to you? Does he seem to wear clothes?" She answered, "Oh no, not clothes like we wear. There seems to be about him a white, beautiful something, so fine and thin and glistening and so white and yet there isn't a fold or thread in it, so it can't be cloth. But it makes him look so lovely."

Her father then quoted from the Psalm "Who coverest thyself with light as with a garment" (104:2). "Oh yes, that's it," she replied.

She often spoke of dying and seemed to have such a sense of the reality of her future life and happiness that she had no fear.

The morning of the day she died she said that soon she would have "a new and beautiful body like Allie's" and begged her mother not to cry. She said that if she had been allowed to grow up, perhaps she might have been a bad woman; and that God knew what was best for her.

In the evening she looked at the clock and said "It's half past eight now; when it is half past eleven Allie will come for me."

At about quarter past eleven she said, "No papa, take me up [in your arms]. Allie has come for me." After her father

116

had taken her into his arms, she wanted to sing. Presently someone said "Call Lulu" [her sister], but Daisy answered "Don't disturb her, she is asleep." (This surely indicated that she was not only rational but thoughtful to the end.) Jus as the hands of the clock pointed to half past eleven, she lifted both arms and said "Come Allie," and drew her last breath.

There was a solemn stillness in the room," her mother wrote. "We couldn't weep, and why should we? . . . As we stood there gazing on her dear face, we felt that the room must be full of angels come to comfort us, for a sweet peace fell upon our spirits" (*Visions*, p. 17-26).

Her body was laid to rest in a beautiful cemetery at Stockton, California under a spreading oak tree. But her spirit joined the other children of whom the poet wrote:

Around the throne of God in heaven
Thousands of children stand,
Children whose sins are all forgiven,
A holy, happy band.

What brought them to that world above,
That heaven so bright and fair,
Where all is peace and joy and love,
How came those children there?

On earth they sought the Savior's grace,
On earth they loved His name;
So now they see His blessed face
And stand before the Lamb.

Singing "Glory, Glory,
Glory be to God on high."

Anne H. Shepherd, 1836

CHAPTER 15

Family Relationships

The greatest consolation of a grieving Christian widow regarding a recently departed believing husband is the hope that "Some day we will be forever united in heaven, in the same loving relationship we had on earth."

A heartbroken mother reassures herself that she will once more clasp her darling child to her heart, never again to be separated.

Because the perpetuation in heaven of family ties is so commonly believed and is such a source of comfort, this chapter may at first seem disappointing, particularly to those recently bereaved. On the other hand, it may be a relief to the second wife or a stepchild or a single person.

Those who have remarried have often wondered, "Will I have two husbands in heaven? How will that work out, for I had loved them both. What about his children and mine? Will they maintain love and loyalty to their own parents?

These and other puzzling questions were very simply answered by Jesus in one broad statement which He made to the Sadducees when they approached Jesus with a concocted problem.

Now there were with us seven brethren; and the first,

when he had married a wife, deceased, and, having no issue, left his wife unto his brother; Likewise the second also, and the third, unto the seventh; And last of all the woman died also. Therefore in the resurrection whose wife shall she be of the seven? for they all had her. Jesus answered and said unto them, Ye do err, not knowing the scriptures, nor the power of God. For in the resurrection they neither marry, nor are given in marriage, but are as the angels of God in heaven. (Matt. 22:25-30)

In the Gospel of Luke the same passage is phrased a little differently.

And Jesus answering said unto them, The children of this world marry, and are given in marriage; But they which shall be accounted worthy to obtain that world, and the resurrection from the dead, neither marry, nor are given in marriage. (20:34-36).

Most Bible scholars interpret these words to mean that affections and relationships will change in the next world.

In her book *To Live Again* Catherine Marshall used the above scriptures for the basis of her conviction that love among relatives in heaven will be of a different nature. With selfishness and possessiveness absent, what remains will be a pure love like that delineated in First Corinthians thirteen.

This does not necessarily mean that when the entire family is finally reunited in heaven that they will neither recognize nor care for each other. In scripture, when the rich man found himself in hell, his concern that his brother should not come into the same place of torment indicated that he still remembered and loved his family (Luke 16:20-31).

Many of those seeing heaven in vision or who had glimpsed the other world just before they died, were lovingly and joyfully met by predeceased loved ones. But the newcomer into paradise would not have been there long before he discovered that though there was still family affection, it was of a different and superior kind, stripped of its exclusiveness.

Elizabeth Bossert said that when she saw one of the patriarchs "I seemed to love him as much as I did my own dear parents and loved ones. In heaven there are no family ties, but all are smiling and happy together" (*My Visit*, pp. 13,14).

Bunyan was informed by his celestial guide, "Here we love the blessed God more than ourselves and one another like ourselves, We here are all the children of one Father and all our brethren are alike dear to us" (*Visions*, p. 24).

Earthly love was meant to last only "until death do us part," at which time the man or woman would then be free even to love and marry another. If then, the family relationship is so temporary, lasting only during earth-life, what should be the attitude of husbands and wives and family members toward each other?

It was God's own idea that through the loving union of man and woman that love should be nourished and that the earth should be replenished. It was and is God's desire that a man love his wife with the same depth and intensity that Christ loved the church, and that the wife reverence her husband (Eph. 5:25). To promote harmony and insure the smooth functioning of the family unit, the Holy Spirit inspired the writers of the scriptures to include various admonitions directed specifically to husbands, wives, children.

But over and above all that stands a command which tells of one kind of love which should have priority over all others: ". . . Thou shalt love the Lord thy God with all thy heart, and with all thy soul, and with all thy mind" (Matt. 22:37-38).

This love and loyalty to God is to be so strong as to eclipse all other relationships, for early in His call to His diciples

Jesus said:

> If any one comes to Me, and does not hate his [own]
> father and mother [that is, in the sense of indifference to
> or relative disregard for them in comparison with his
> attitude toward God] and [likewise] his wife and
> children and brothers and sisters, [yes] and even his
> own life also, he cannot be My disciple. (Luke 14:26,
> TAB)

Those who so loved God and so put Him first in their
heart's affections would be fulfilling what Jesus called the
first and great commandment.

According to this, then, we would want to make the order
of priorities like this: God first, my spouse and family and
relatives next.

But this is not so. For besides the first and great
commandment, Jesus added another: "And the second is like
unto it, Thou shalt love thy neighbour as thyself" (Matt.
22:39). The priority list now would read: God first, others
second, myself (and my relatives) last. Right?

We have been talking about family *affections*—our
personal feelings to them. But what about family
relationships? How are we to consider them?

From the human standpoint, Jesus made it clear. When
the multitude told Him that His mother and brethren
desired to speak to Him, He said,

> . . . Who is my mother? and who are my brethren?
> And he stretched forth his hand toward his disciples,
> and said, Behold my mother and my brethren.
>
> For whosoever shall do the will of my Father which is
> in heaven, the same is my brother, and sister, and
> mother. (Matt. 12:48-50)

In telling us to love God supremely and to love our
neighbor as ourselves, the Lord established a new and
superior order of relationships: the family of God. Several
scriptures refer specifically to this spiritual family.

Of whom the whole family in heaven and earth is named.
(Eph. 3:15)

That . . . he might gather together in one all things in
Christ, both which are in heaven and which are on
earth. (Eph. 1:10)

Now therefore ye are . . . fellow citizens with the
saints, and of the household of God. (Eph. 2:19)

As we have therefore opportunity, let us do good unto
all men, especially unto them who are of the household
of faith. (Gal. 6:10)

In this new family relationship—which we enter through
the new birth—we have God as our Father, Jesus Christ as
our Elder Brother, and all reborn ones as brothers and
sisters in Christ.

When Bunyan was in heaven he learned from one of its
residents, "Here all human relations cease and are all
swallowed up in God, who alone is the great Father of this
heavenly family. Since I have put off the body, I have with
that too put off all relations in the flesh. Nor have I here any
relatives else. We are all children of one Father and servants
of one Master, in whose blessed service is our perfect
freedom" (*Visions*, p. 33).

As we are commanded to love God supremely, so we are
now exhorted to love His children, the members of the new
spiritual family. "And this commandment have we from him,
That he who loveth God love his brother also" (1 John 4:21).
". . . See that ye love one another with a pure heart
fervently" (1 Pet. 1:22).

We are even told that we must love our spiritual brethren
with the same kind of love that Christ loved us, so that "we
ought to lay down our lives for the brethren" (1 John 3:16).

Love is the greatest force on earth. It is that which binds
together a man and woman, children and parents, brothers
and sisters. Yet, because of man's weak and sinful nature,
human love has its boundaries and limitations. This is

evidenced by a divorce rate of one in four marriages, by friction and bitterness and sometimes even lawsuits within many families. For example, two elderly widows, sisters, finding living alone too costly, tried living together. After less than a year they discovered they could not get along, so they separated, choosing rather loneliness and the extra expense to disharmony with a blood relative!

Many families and couples do enjoy a close and beautiful relationship. Yet, when ties are severed by death, they learn a curious truth: that after even so short a span as a year's time, they have forgotten the excruciating pain of the separation. With further passage of time, even the memory of that loved one becomes dim and almost fades.

Because life is like that, we ought not regret too much that human relationships are not perpetuated in heaven. Knowing the inadequacy of natural love, the Lord has provided a higher and better relationship—fellowship with the spiritual family of God.

While we are on earth and in the body, the two families run concurrently—the natural and the spiritual. But though *natural* family ties will be severed at death, the *spiritual* is destined to continue in heaven through eternity.

This relationship will be one of exceeding joy, as Bunyan was informed:

"Here we see not only our elder brother Christ but also our friends and relations. Here we communicate the purest pleasure to each other, an unfeigned ardent love uniting all our pure society. Here everyone is perfectly amiable and perfectly enamoured with each other. And oh how happy this state of love!" (*Visions*, p. 30).

A song which has been recently popular in evangelical churches is "I'm so glad I'm a part of the family of God." I don't know whether we will sing this song in heaven, but we will most surely be expressing its sentiments.

SECTION TWO

Preparing for Heaven

The previous chapters have been comparatively light reading. We now come to the most important chapters of this book. They contain "meat" which will appeal mainly to those who, rather than merely being interested in knowing about heaven, desire to *do* something about being fully prepared for it. It is the latter kind of readers who will more likely fulfill God's eternal purpose in their lives.

CHAPTER 16

Building on the Foundation

I hope you are convinced that heaven is a real and superlatively wonderful place, and that any fear of dying you may have had is now replaced by joyful anticipation, provided you are a Christian.

I don't mean Christian as distinguished from heathen, but Christian in the scriptural sense, and that is one who has repented of his sins and received forgiveness, and one who has committed himself to the Lord Jesus Christ as his Savior in a personal way. By choosing to follow the Lord, you have made man's most important decision; you have made sure of your eternal destiny.

But is the ultimate of God's plan over man to be saved from hell and to go to heaven? Just that and nothing more?

In *Caught Up To Heaven,* a booklet about happenings when Mrs. Carol Hooley was taken to heaven, she told of her reaction upon seeing an uncle who had recently died and, she had assumed, was not a Christian.

"For some reason, I wanted to turn my face," she wrote, "for my uncle was not robed like the others about him. It wasn't the feeling of embarrassment from looking on one who seemed naked, but . . . that my uncle had just barely made it into heaven.

"When I returned [to earth] I learned that he had accepted Jesus Christ as his personal Savior just prior to his death . . .

"My uncle received the gift of eternal life the same as any other believer because salvation is by grace, not works. Yet he did not live a victorious life in Christ here on earth; he did not build upon the foundation of faith in Christ.

"He waited until the very end of his life to commit himself to Jesus Christ. . . . I saw a definite distinction between my uncle and those who had lived a consecrated Christian life" (p. 12).

Deathbed conversions are fairly common, but few Christians regard them in the right perspective. If the relatives of this uncle were like most believers, they would have been jubilant because "Uncle made it just before he died, praise the Lord!"

In one sense, their triumph would be justified because one more victim had been pulled from the brink of hell, to turn Satan's glee at the last moment into rage. In heaven everyone rejoices when a redeemed sinner arrives, even if he had been snatched as a brand from the burning.

But that does not tell the whole story.

No one would know as well as the Lord himself and those who had already spent some time in heaven what it means for a person to arrive in such a state of spiritual infancy.

In a passage in 1 Corinthians 3, the Apostle Paul makes it clear that the person who enters heaven without having built upon the foundation of his faith in Jesus ". . . he *shall suffer loss:* but he himself shall be saved; yet so as by fire" (v. 15, italics mine). This tragedy could happen to others than last-minute converts. The context of this passage describes various kinds of *Christians:* those who built upon the foundation with gold, silver, precious stones and those who built with wood, hay, stubble (1 Cor. 3:11-13).

The apostle warns them to "take heed how ye build" upon the foundation, because rewards in heaven will be given only to those who earn them.

Some Christians piously murmur, "I'm not concerned about rewards in heaven; I will be satisfied just to get there." They almost roll their eyes heavenward and sag with humility while making this pronouncement. Nothing in scripture endorses such "humility," for it is God himself who cares very deeply whether His children get through the school of life with an A or a D on their report cards.

The Christian who is too busy to engage in his church's soul-winning efforts, but who spends hours before the TV; who has plenty of time for hobbies, but can barely spare one night a week for the house of God; who seldom speaks to God in his prayer closet, but endlessly chats with friends on the phone, undoubtedly will get to heaven. But it is questionable whether he will be welcomed by a thirty-piece angelic brass band!

The Apostle Peter says that those who are neither "barren nor unfruitful" in the knowledge of the Lord will find the gates wide open: "For so an entrance shall be ministered unto you *abundantly* into the everlasting kingdom of our Lord and Savior Jesus Christ" (2 Pet. 1:8, 11, italics mine).

The aim of my Christian life is to prepare me, not merely to get into heaven by the skin of my teeth, but to arrive there in as developed and mature a state as the Holy Spirit can possibly get me to be.

One reason why many Christians are not overly concerned about the quality and depth of their Christian lives is a gross misconception about what heaven will be like. They vaguely imagine that all the inhabitants thereof will be a sort of happy, homogeneous mass of anonymities, each an exact duplicate of the other. However, in the next few chapters we will be showing by scripture and vision that there will be great differences among the saints in heaven.

We can be introduced to this concept by relating what was revealed to Sundar Singh during one of his visits to heaven. "In it [Paradise] are innumerable planes of existence and the soul is conducted to that plane for which its progress in the world has fitted it" (*Visions*, p. 14).

God intends that immediately after conversion Christians should begin the lifetime process of building upon the foundation of their faith in Christ, because the progress made on earth will determine eternal destiny.

I cannot stress strongly enough the importance of the quality of one's Christian life on earth, for it will make all the difference in eternity.

This was shown to Mrs. Booth Tucker of the Salvation Army, during a vision in which she conversed with her deceased mother.

In the course of the vision, Mrs. Tucker had confided to her mother's spirit that because of her many difficulties, she secretly longed to join her in heaven. Her mother then spoke to her of the great value in heaven that is given to life and its opportunities; adding finally that "Its moments, its very moments, I see to be worth countless millions now."

Mrs. Tucker said she did not remember half the words of her mother, but knew that she was so deeply impressed with the "inestimable privileges of time" that she became ashamed that she ever had longed for heaven.

Toward the close of the vision, her mother said "Fight the fight; the sympathy of Christ is always with you. *Every effort you make is heaping up treasure for you in Heaven*" (*Life of Mrs. Booth* by W.T. Stead [New York: Salvation Army, date] p. 235-238, italics mine).

This vision became an important element in launching Mrs. Tucker into her successful ministry in the Salvation Army.

How brief life is, but how important in relation to eternity! It provides the school in which we learn and from which we should graduate qualified to serve forever in the life which is to come.

When we realize that so much must be done in so short a time, we cry with the Psalmist, "So teach us to number our days, that we may apply our hearts unto wisdom" (Ps. 90:12).

CHAPTER 17

The Eternal Purpose

It began with a plan.

Silently, majestically, age upon age, myriads of galaxies moved through the vast and limitless cosmos called the universe.

From somewhere, amid an immense blaze of glory, there flowed a gentle but powerful force called Love. And His name was God.

And God said,

"Let us make man in our image, after our likeness," and let us give him dominion over earth, and let us walk with him forever (Gen. 1:26).

Since God had always lived in the perfect fellowship of Father, Son and Holy Spirit, no one really knows why He wanted something more, why He wanted man.

Perhaps the Father had so much love, He had to share it with a being He would call man.

Since this man would have to be someone to whom He could relate on an "equal" basis, He created one perfect in character, free in will and eternal in being.

With this man God walked in the cool of the day and to this man He entrusted the care of the world He had made for him.

We have no record of how long God walked with Adam and Eve in the garden of Eden, which is also paradise. It may have been for centuries.

Then came the woeful day when God's enemy Satan entered the garden to destroy the plan.

Knowing beforehand that this would happen, God called upon "the Lamb slain from the foundation of the world" to come to the rescue (Rev. 13:8). His mission regarding man would be twofold:

1. To save His people from their sins.
2. To restore them to the "original."

Through salvation, believers would be eligible for entrance into heaven. Through the process of restoration, believers would qualify themselves for rewards, capacities to relate to God and positions of service in heaven.

Because the task of first saving man, then changing him, was such a large and important one, God entrusted it to the Holy Spirit himself.

God had to alter His plans and purposes over man. He did not abandon the original plan, but made eternally significant changes.

Early in their history, man understood the cost of his sin. Now that he had become mortal, his stay on earth would be a brief seventy or eighty years. Beginning with Abraham, God's people knew that ". . . here we have no continuing city, but we seek one to come" that they were merely strangers on earth, foreigners, pilgrims, looking for a city which hath foundations, in which all the children of God would find permanent residence, in their Father's house (Gen. 23:4, Ps. 39:12, Phil. 3:20, Heb. 11:13-16).

Now, because of the extreme brevity of life, God's

purpose for man would have to extend far beyond earth. God therefore devised two plans over each individual:

Plan 1: What man should be and do during his temporary sojourn on earth.

Plan 2: What man should be and do during his permanent residence in the world to come.

Earth would still figure in God's plan. But it would now be the environment, the school, the training place, yea, the crucible in which the Holy Spirit would fulfill the chief purpose of God.

From the time that each individual becomes a member of the household of God, the Holy Spirit begins the work of fulfilling the dual plans: the *earthly*, for the purpose of the *heavenly*. "We are assured and know that [God being a partner in their labor], all things work together and are [fitting into a plan] for good to those who love God and are called according to [His] design and purpose" (Rom. 8:28, TAB).

By this God means that all He allows to happen to each of His children is meant for his good. The scripture which immediately follows this passage begins with "for," making the sequence of thought clear that the "good" primarily refers to that which is spiritual and eternal. "For whom he did foreknow, he also did predestinate *to be conformed to the image of his Son*, that he might be the firstborn among many brethren" (Rom. 8:29, italics mine).

This brings us back to the early counsels of God when the Father said to the Son "Let us make man in our image and after our likeness." This time, however, it would not be the original creation, but a *restoration* to that original pattern.

His design now was that He might have in heaven many sons like unto the Son to whom He could relate and with whom He could share the responsibilities of the work of His eternal Kingdom, in heaven.

The task of maturing God's newborn sons was begun by the Apostle Paul, who said "So we preach Christ to everyone. With all possible wisdom, we warn and teach them in order to *bring each individual into God's presence as a mature individual* in union with Christ" (Colossians 1:28 TEV, italics mine).

It is therefore the solemn responsibility of the ministry to be dedicated to a twofold goal:

1. Bringing men to salvation.
2. Bringing men to maturity.

This, then, would fulfill the eternal plan and purpose of God.

This is what life on earth is all about.

CHAPTER 18

Rewards

What I have said in the previous chapter is of utmost importance: That God has over us an eternal plan, part of which is that He has predestined us to be conformed to the image of Christ. His reasons are (1) that He may have in heaven many sons like the Son, compatible to himself, and (2) that He may have sons qualified to share with Him His work in the next world.

This invests life with an awesome importance: for what I am and what I do in this life will determine what I will be and will do in the next life.

In his book *There's a New World Coming*, Hal Lindsey expresses a similar thought: "We need to realize that we're preparing our 'garments for eternity' right now. From the shabby Christian lives that some people live, it looks like there will be some 'heavenly hippies.' It's better to be a hippy in Heaven than not be there at all, but it's better to be a bride adorned to her fullest with a garment that befits the bride of a royal King" (p. 257).

Scriptures showing that the quality of our lives on earth will be reflected in heaven fall into several categories:

Rewards
Promises to overcomers
Parables
Crowns

The average reader of a book like this skips over quoted scriptures or reads them hurriedly. For that reason I will briefly mention scriptures here. Those who care to delve more deeply may easily do so with their own Bibles.

One general scripture which amply covers the subject is ". . . godliness is profitable unto all things, having promise of the life that now is, *and of that which is to come*" (1 Tim. 4:8, italics mine). If you have read this verse rapidly, please read it again and again, especially the last phrase. It has a vital message for Christians.

Scriptures on Rewards

One amazing thing about God is that not only will He take us to heaven, but that afterward He will also give us rewards. ". . . Verily there is a reward for the righteous" (Ps. 58:11). Rewards are, of course, given to those earning them.

In heaven there will be no TV giveaways such as a trip to Hawaii for naming ten vegetables in ten seconds. At Sunday school picnics children receive pencils and toys as awards. But for dedicated labor such as outstanding salesmanship, an insurance company will give a substantial promotion.

The Apostle Paul said that ". . . every man shall receive his own reward according to his own labor" (1 Cor. 3:8).

Rewards seem to be given primarily, but not exclusively for what we *do*. Mentioned in the Bible are rewards for (1) diligently seeking God (Heb. 11:6), (2) fasting and praying (Matt. 6:6,16,18), (3) giving alms and not bragging about it (Matt. 6:4), (4) ministering to "one of the least of his brethren" (Matt. 10:42).

Countless Christians are God's drudges. They drive the

church bus, fold endless stacks of Sunday school papers, serve in church nurseries, take discouraged women to the welfare department. Others labor overseas, trek through wild jungles to reach one obscure village, or burn or freeze on mission fields.

After her visit to heaven, Elizabeth Bossert wrote ". . . The giving of little things . . . is soon forgotten by you. But it is all recorded, and rewards are awaiting you. If our small deeds are rewarded, what must be our reward for the larger sacrifices we make for the cause of Christ! . . . Do not miss them at any cost, for they are wonderful" (*My Visit*, p. 14). "For God is not unrighteous to forget your work and labor of love which you have showed toward his name in that ye have ministered to the saints and do minister" (Heb. 6:10).

Blessings Promised to Overcomers
To overcomers in each of the seven churches mentioned in Revelation 1-3 are promised rewards. Interpretations as to exact meaning vary, but it seems clear that something special will happen in the next world to those who qualify as overcomers. "Him that overcometh will I make a pillar in the temple of my god . . ." (Rev. 3:12). "To him that overcometh will I grant to sit with me in my throne, even as I also overcame and am set down with my Father in his throne" (Rev. 3:21). The implication is that overcomers will be especially close to Jesus ("sit with me") and that they will share a special place of authority ("on my throne").

Gordon Lindsay said, regarding positions in heaven, "There will be great differences in rank and position of the saved in the next age" (*Paradise, Abode of the Righteous Dead* [Dallas: Voice of Healing, n.d.], p. 28).

He also says, "Although there will be various rewards of the faithful, the most important reward will be the position of nearness to Christ in all His activities during the ages to come. All will see Him, all will be known of Him; but there will be those who are closer to Him than others" (ibid).

We have no problem in understanding, at least to a degree, what special closeness to God would mean. But what it means to share with Him a special place of authority, we can only conjecture.

A number of Christian writers agree with the suggestion made by Hal Lindsey that "It is possible that there is intelligent life on other planets, which God will reveal to us in eternity. We may rule over them" (*New World*, p. 297).

Many astronomers share this opinion. They say that even within our own galaxy, which consists of about ten million planetary systems similar to our own, there might be planets capable of sustaining life. Not only within our own Milky Way Galaxy, but also among the other two million galaxies occupying space.

In any event, whatever the nature of the rulership with Christ in His kingdom may be, apparently not all will be eligible.

Parables

The scriptures say that the following relate to the kingdom of heaven: The parables of the pounds, the talents and the vineyard.

In the parable of the pounds (Luke 19:12-27) the nobleman gave each of his ten servants one pound. The one who gained ten more was granted authority over ten cities; the servant who gained five received authority over five cities. Both were praised for faithful service, but received authority in proportion to their gain.

In the parable of the talents (Matt. 25:14-30) the Lord distributed five, two and one talents to his servants "according to their several ability." The five-talent man who gained five and the two-talent man who gained two were

140

equally commended. The unprofitable servant who hid his talent was severely reprimanded for being wicked and slothful. (It seems that God has nothing good to say about laziness.)

In the parable of the vineyard (Matt. 20:1-16), the householder hired laborers at the beginning of the day, also at the third, sixth and even up to the eleventh hour. At the day's end, he paid them all the same amount. A superficial reading of this parable has given rise to the mistaken interpretation that this means all Christians will receive equal rewards in heaven. This parable indeed contains difficulties which have troubled commentators in all ages of the church. Let us attempt to understand it.

In the previous verses (chapter 19) Jesus promised the rich young ruler rewards in heaven if he would sell his possessions and give to the poor (v. 21). After which Peter said, "Behold we have forsaken all, what shall we have?" (v. 27). Jesus replied that he and others making similar sacrifices would receive authority in the next world (v. 28). Both passages, interestingly, conclude with words to the effect that the first shall be last, and the last first (19:30; 20:16).

It seems evident that Jesus means that rewards will depend not upon *length* of service, but *quality*. In other words, a fully committed new convert can attain to the same degree of growth and thereby earn the same reward as the one saved for a lifetime.

In every church we find saints who, after fifty years, are more dedicated than ever. There will also be some old-timers who appear to be just living on past experiences. But the growing church will also have new Christians so wholly committed that if they continue, they will be numbered among the last who become first.

Significant words at the end of this parable seem to wrap

up the lesson. "For many be called but few chosen" (or choice ones) (Matt. 20:16).

Several scholars say this indicates two classes of Christians: the called and the chosen. Revelation 17:14 adds a third: "they that are with Him are called and chosen and faithful."

Out of the multitude of those who are called, emerges a smaller company of the chosen (or choice ones). This narrows to a still smaller company: the faithful. If there remains any doubt in our minds, it should be settled by the words of Jesus, "For the Son of man shall come in the glory of his Father with his angels; and then he shall reward every man according to his works" (Matt. 16:27).

Crowns

Various crowns are given as a reward: (1) the crown of life, for faithfulness (Rev. 2:10); (2) the crown of righteousness, to those who love His appearing (2 Tim 4:8); (3) the incorruptible crown, for striving for the mastery (1 Cor. 9:25); (4) the crown of glory, promised to faithful elders (1 Pet. 5:4).

Whatever the nature of these crowns, I doubt that the moment a Christian arrives in heaven that he will be instructed to stand in line and wait for his crown to be handed to him. For not all will receive one. In ancient times crowns—more precisely, laurel wreaths—were awarded to the athletes who won the contests in which they competed. Surely those wreaths would have meant little had they been handed out to every contestant.

Although the scripture says much about rewards and blessings promised to the faithful, to the overcomers and to the godly, we are not told exactly what they will be. Several who had visions or who had visited heaven mentioned that although the dwelling places were all attractive, some were far more beautiful than others. Rewards are also promised which are less "tangible." One verse says "I am thy . . . exceeding great reward" (Gen. 15:1).

I believe that Revelation 3:21, which says that overcomers will "sit with him" implies that the rewards will be twofold: special nearness to God in fellowship and close association with Him in eternal service.

Dr. Robert Frost says, "Many of the Lord's parables indicate we are to be laying up eternal treasure in heaven (Matt. 6:19-20). It is at the level of our spirit-soul life that we become conformed into His image. It is that picture which determines our reward in heaven. Rewards will, without doubt, be related to our capacity to enjoy and express the life of Christ throughout the ages" (*Set My Spirit Free*, p. 192).

Unless we are diligent we will either receive lesser rewards or lose them altogether. The third chapter of 1 Corinthians says that those who build with gold, silver and precious stones will be rewarded. Those building with wood, hay, stubble will be saved, yet so as by fire, *but they will suffer loss*. In 2 John 8 we read another solemn warning: "Look to yourselves that we *lose not* those things which we have wrought [margin, gained] but that we receive a full reward."

CHAPTER 19

Growth: God's Great Project

It was a perfect day and a perfect place for the family reunion—a sunny July afternoon, in the lake area of the forest preserve. Everyone was especially happy because the oldest in the clan, Great-grandfather Olson had come from Sweden for the occasion. He had about him an air of European hardiness: pink cheeks, thick white hair, booming voice, keen mind and a remarkably steady gait for a man of ninety. Naturally, he was the central figure. From time to time various relatives clustered about him, receiving his affectionate attention.

"And you're Helge's son, ten years old. I saw you climb that tree—just like I used to when I was your age."

"So you are Billie, and you are going into first grade this fall. Wonderful! Now let me hear the ABC's."

"Alice. Just two little years. Here, sit on grandpa's foot; I'll swing you like we do in Sweden. Up we go!"

"And this is the baby. Let me hold him. Kitchie, kitchie, koo. . . . Now, now, don't cry. Grandpa's wrinkled old face frightens you. Here, mama, take the little darling."

Great-grandfather communicated with the young ones on their levels. With the high school and college age young people he talked about boy and girl friends, school and future professions. It was all enjoyable. But most gratifying was his association with the adults—the parents and grandparents of the group. With them he talked as man to man, in the fellowship of kindred minds, developed and mature. This was true rapport.

Likewise, some day all of God's children will be gathered in heaven for a family reunion, to at last fulfill His great desire, "that where I am, there ye may be also" (John 14:3). Jesus will have already come to earth and returned to heaven with His church. School days, testing days, growing days are ended and life in the new world begins. John describes the scene: "After this I beheld and lo a great multitude which no man could number, of all nations and kindreds and people and tongues stood before the throne and before the Lamb, clothed with white robes and palms in their hands" (Rev. 7:9).

Those who have attended large international conferences can well imagine the scene of thousands upon thousands of saints gathered from the four corners of the earth. Present will be aborigines from Australia, natives from South American jungles, Eskimos from Alaska, high caste Hindus from India, the Russian peasant, the German professor, the American housewife—all members of the family of God. Most of these will have already been in heaven, some for centuries; others will have newly arrived as the last company at the coming of the Lord.

When that great and glorious homecoming meeting is ended and the saints begin to disperse, slowly pouring out of the vast hall, *what will happen next?* It is possible that the angels of the Lord will commence to "direct traffic." Those who have been in heaven for some time will of course have no orientation problem; but the newcomers would need to be shown where to go.

Will an archangel stand on a high platform and with bullhorn announce: "Africans this way, Asians to the left, Europeans to the right? Or will he shout, "Baptists here, Methodists there, Charismatics this way?" Or, "Those who have been saved for less than a year, or for ten years or fifteen—this way and that"? Or will everybody be directed to the *same part* of heaven?

Differences of Location

As I have already said, a number of scriptures indicate or imply that not all of the redeemed are going to be in the same location. Jesus said that in His Father's house there were many "dwelling places" (John 14:2 TAB). The Apostle Paul mentions differing rewards and varying degrees of glory (1 Cor. 3:12-15; 15:38-42).

During one of his visits to heaven, Sadhu Singh learned that "in Heaven there are innumerable planes of existence," and also that "there are grades upon grades, right up to the higher heavens" (*Visions*, pp. 14,27). Others having visions were also informed concerning the different groupings and placements of the saints.

Basis for the Allocations

What is the determining factor on which these various placements are made? Obviously it is not race or religion, education or culture or wealth. The qualifications are, of course, moral and spiritual. In the previous chapter we have already read that rewards will be apportioned to each individual for his deeds and for faithfulness to personal potential.

Likewise, those will be granted special places of nearness to Jesus and special kinds of service in heaven who have qualified for them by the depth and degree of their spiritual growth or maturity. This is suggested by the whole tenor of the New Testament and by a number of specific references such as the promises to the overcomers and the profit of godliness.

This position is confirmed by what Sadhu Singh learned while he was in heaven. "The place of residence is appointed for each soul in the plane for which his spiritual development has fitted him" (*Visions*, p. 31).

Writing in the *Pentecostal Evangel* (January 8, 1976), J. Bashford Bishop stated: "Those who give their lives to Christ and lose themselves in Him and in His cause are the happiest here on this earth, *and they will enter into a life of infinitely greater fulness with Christ in His Kingdom*" (italics mine).

If God purposes to restore man into His original creation, then we can understand why God is so concerned over the spiritual growth and maturity of His children. I am acquainted with a physician and his wife who have three sons. Two of them are retarded. Of course they love the deficient sons, in whom they see physical evidence of family identity. But only to the normal son, after he had achieved maturity could they entrust responsibilities and only with him can they have real fellowship.

No parents, having brought a child into the world, can ever feel satisfied that they have accomplished their purpose. Their goal is not the birth of a child, but his development into a responsible adult who will fill his place in the world of competent men and to whom they can personally now relate on an equal basis.

Therefore the heavenly Parent, knowing that growth takes time, is eager that every child of His, newly born into His family, should at once ". . . as newborn babes desire the sincere milk of the word that ye may grow thereby" (1 Pet. 2:2). Unfortunately, God is quite aware that not all of His children will fully mature. The Apostle Paul chided some

Hebrew Christians with:

You have been Christians a long time now, and you ought to be teaching others, but instead you have dropped back to the place where you need someone to teach you all over again the very first principles in God's Word. You are like babies who can drink only milk, not old enough for solid food. And when a person is still living on milk it shows he isn't very far along in the Christian life, and doesn't know much about the difference between right and wrong. He is still a baby-Christian! You will never be able to eat solid spiritual food and understand the deeper things of God's Word until you become better Christians and learn right from wrong by practicing doing right. (Heb. 5:12-14, TLB)

In an article on spiritual growth Ralph Mahoney wrote: "Three Greek words are used to denote the Eastern concept of growth. The first is 'teknion' meaning an infant or a little child. The second is 'teknon' meaning an adolescent child. The third is 'huios' meaning a son" (*World Map Digest*, Jan.-Feb., 1969). Among God's family members will be found those in varying degrees of spiritual growth. Perhaps one of the Lord's great disappointments is that He already has in His eternal kingdom and will have many others, those who are still babes or children or adolescents, but comparatively few spiritual adults.

So desirous is God over the growth of His children that we are told He gave to the church apostles, prophets, evangelists, pastors and teachers for the purpose of perfecting the saints. "Till we all come . . . unto a perfect man, unto the measure of the stature [age, margin] of the fulness of Christ. That we henceforth be no more children . . . But . . . may grow up into him in all things . . ." (Eph. 4:13-15).

Many Christians consider preoccupation with one's own spirituality to be unwholesome self-centeredness. To them, Christian growth is a kind of afterthought, to be stressed only on special occasions like deeper life conferences or to be taught in poorly attended, small, midweekly Bible classes. Others say that to be striving for rewards or better places in heaven or greater closeness to God denotes a lamentable competiveness. That is looking at it from the human viewpoint. But how does God see it?

God himself is the orginator of this whole thing. He is the one whose ambition, goal, plan is involved. This is *His* dream. For even before man was created, God had already predestined him to be conformed to the image of His Son. Just how God really feels about this maturing of His children is expressed in the cry of St. Paul: "My little children, of whom I travail in birth again until Christ be formed in you. . ." (Gal. 4:19). The travail of God is also shown in Romans 8:26. "The Spirit itself maketh intercession for us with groanings which cannot be uttered." This has often been interpreted to mean "travail for the salvation of souls." However, it takes only slight attention to the context to see what it is saying.

Likewise, the Spirit also helpeth our infirmities: for we know not what we should pray for as we ought: but the Spirit itself maketh intercession for us with groanings which cannot be uttered. And he that searcheth the hearts knoweth what is the mind of the Spirit, because he maketh intercession for the saints, according to the will of God. (Rom. 8:26-27)

Please note: the intercession is *for the saints*.

That weighty passage in Ephesians 6 about spiritual warfare is concluded with the following plea: "Praying always with all prayer and supplication in the Spirit, and watching thereunto with all perseverance and supplication for all saints" (v. 18). Please note again, it is *for the saints.*

I hope you're not skipping or skimming over these scriptures. If you are, please read those passages again. Here's another one, in which the writer to the Ephesians tells us that Christ gave himself for the church in order to "sanctify and cleanse it with the washing of water by the word. That he might present it to himself a glorious church, not having spot, or wrinkle, or any such thing; but that it should be holy and without blemish" (5:27).

God is concerned with a great deal more than *how many* He can get into heaven. He is indeed interested in numbers. For we read that in heaven the angels who control the "heavenly computers" rejoice over every additional sinner whose repentance they register (Luke 15:10).

But would it seem inconceivable to you that God may also have assigned to some angels "computers" which make entries of spiritual development? We are told that "then they that feared the LORD spake often one to another: and the LORD hearken, and heard it, and a book of remembrance was written before him for them that feared the LORD, and that thought upon his name" (Mal. 3:16). Could it not be that there is joy in the presence of the angels of God over every Christian who grows steadily? Is the potter observing the vessel take shape? Do parents rejoice when their children bring home a progress report which indicates improvements in various areas?

Although they have not been the most numerous of His children, God has always had throughout the centuries those who were willing to pay the price of spiritual maturity. As a man seeks for treasure, so the Lord seeks for such. "For the eyes of the Lord run to and fro throughout the whole earth to show himself strong in behalf of those whose heart is blameless toward him" (2 Chron. 16:9, TAB).

In the Old Testament we have such men as Noah, Enoch,

Abraham who did the will of God and who walked in close fellowship with Him. Gordon Lindsay speaks of the New Testament saints: "When the Lord was on earth, there were three disciples closest to Him—Peter, James and John. Then there was another group not quite so close, and these nine made up the remainder of the group. Also there were the seventy to whom He gave special power to heal and to cast out devils.

"There was another group who were present at the Upper Room at the time the Holy Spirit fell on the day of Pentecost. There were 500 disciples to whom Christ revealed Himself in His resurrected form. Thus we see that when Jesus was here on earth, each follower fell into a special group or classification. So it will be in the world to come" (*Paradise*, p. 28). The pages of religious history are adorned with the names of such saints as Francis of Assisi, George Fox, A.B. Simpson and many others who wholly followed the Lord.

Why is God so deeply interested in the growth of His children? What is the reason for His unceasing quest for true saints? It is because He wants them to fit into, not simply his earthly plan, but his eternal plan over their lives. That is why it is infinitely important to God that His children develop abilities and capacities while on earth.

After Julia Ruopp had her remarkable experience of seeing into heaven, she reappraised her life in terms of eternal values. "I believe there is a comparison to be drawn between birth of the spirit and childbirth. We know that if the infant has ready the equipment for breathing—nostrils, lungs and air passages, then he is able to live in a world of air. However, if the fetal development is incomplete or faulty, he is unprepared for a world where breathing is a necessity. In like manner, in this life, if one's soul or spirit remains undernourished, underdeveloped and unrelated, then it cannot enter into or function freely in the highest form of life to which it is capable of attaining. It came to me with certainty then that one *began* there in the next world where he *leaves off here* this life.

"And if one is unprepared or unable to 'breathe' the atmosphere of that state, or bear the light of a more intense or luminous quality, then one would have to go through a period of waiting or adjustment. This seemed to give a deeper meaning to suffering, to all experience and to one's everyday relationships. *Not to grow spiritually seemed to me then and still does the real death of the individual.* [Italics mine.] Thus, I believe that my brief glimpse through the window of heaven was a flash of revelation about the meaning of life itself" (*Window*, pp.30-31).

CHAPTER 20

Growing Pains, Part One

Since the growth of His children into the likeness of His Son is God's prime objective, we ought to find out how to achieve this. A good way would be to examine the factors involved in the growth of Jesus from infancy to maturity. The Bible tells us "And the child grew, and waxed strong in spirit, filled with wisdom: and the grace of God was upon him" (Luke 2:40). "And Jesus increased in wisdom and stature, and in favor with God and man" (Luke 2:52).

These statements provide us with three broad divisions for a study of Jesus' development:

1. His relations with God.
2. His relations with people.
3. His relations with himself—His inner life.

Later, there had to be included a fourth:

4. His relations to Satan.

The environment for this growth was first, His home in Nazareth, then the outside world. Under these conditions and in these four areas Jesus so grew that God would say of Him ". . . This is my beloved Son, in whom I am well pleased" (Matt. 3:17).

A closer look at how Jesus grew reveals principles we can

155

apply to our own progress.

1. Jesus' relation to God

    He frequently withdrew to pray.

    He was committed to do God's will, not His own.

    He was completely dependent upon God.

    He was filled with the Spirit.

2. Jesus' relation to people

    Jesus loved people.

    He served them.

    Above all, He became their Savior.

3. Jesus' relation to Satan

    Jesus overcame Satan on a personal basis in areas representing the world, the flesh and the devil (Matt. 4:1-11). He also overcame Satan as part of His mission: ". . . For this purpose the Son of God was manifested, that he might destroy the works of the devil" (1 John 3:8).

4. Jesus' relation to himself or his inner life

    Beside some of the Messianic Psalms, we have only a few scriptures which provide direct insight into Jesus' inner life, some of which are:

    "And he went down with them [Joseph and Mary] and came to Nazareth and was subject unto them . . ." (Luke 2:51). "Though he were a Son, yet learned he obedience by the things which he suffered" (Heb. 5:8). "Ye have not yet resisted unto blood, striving against sin" (Heb. 12:4).

    The thirty years of home life in Nazareth must have afforded Jesus with the same opportunities for overcoming that it does in every household. Later, during His public ministry, He was also exposed to innumerable trying conditions with His oft-unperceptive disciples, the fawning or pressing multitudes and His malicious enemies. Since he was tempted just as we are, then He could have yielded to anger, pride, harshness, resentments, impatience, criticism —everything. Yet in His human nature, He overcame and remained without sin. "And being made perfect, he became the author of eternal salvation unto all them that obey him" (Heb. 5:9). The patterns left us by the Lord Jesus serve as guides for our growth in the same four areas.

My Growth in Relation to God

In this regard, an almost forgotten song conveys to us a pungent message for today:

> Take time to be holy, the world rushes on.
> Spend much time in secret with Jesus alone.
> By looking to Jesus, like Him thou shalt be.
> Thy friends in thy conduct His likeness shall see.
>
> [W.D. Longstaff]

Several scriptures show us that Jesus' life was undergirded with two kinds of prayer: intercession and communion. The first relates to an important service we can render towards people; the second, to something so sacred that we almost must whisper it—our personal intimacy with God in the holy of holies.

It is in these two areas that much of the church is woefully deficient. Consider intercessory prayer. In most churches, the most poorly attended service by far is the prayer meeting. And even then, what it really amounts to is a midweekly meeting with a few prayers tacked on the end. Most of these prayers are very brief, a few exceedingly long—traversing from Jerusalem to the uttermost parts of the earth. But real intercession, such as described in the book *Rees Howells: Intercessor* and the books on prayer by E.M. Bounds, is rare.

What takes place in public prayer meetings is usually a reflection of what happens in the "prayer closet" of the individual Christian. If he should devote a half hour or so to "prayer," it is mostly taken up with reading a few chapters in the Bible, maybe something from a spiritual book and then offering up a few short petitions for various needs.

This is the residue of that almost extinct breed which we used to call prayer warriors—those saints who knew how to lay hold of God, sometimes praying all night like Jacob. Prayers, intercessions, supplications, fastings, prayer in the Holy Ghost—these are all Bible expressions. But how many know about these kinds of prayer?

Thank God, some of it is being restored to the church during the current renewal; but there remains much need for growth in the area of intercessory prayer.

While we admit to the scarcity of real intercessors, we must also acknowledge the dearth of those who have learned to sit at the feet of Jesus, just to love and worship Him. This is the kind of T.M. the church needs—true meditation—times of silent adoration and communion with God.

Sadly, many vigorous Christians, who even though they may acknowledge the need for closer fellowship with God, inadvertently fail to "be still and know that I am God (Ps. 46:10). The reason: they feel it is being too "mystical." By avoiding both the practice and the advocacy of this kind of prayer, Christians and preachers are driving many people, who are truly seeking communion with God, into Transcendental Meditation centers.

They are also depriving themselves of a very important means of becoming fitted for greater capacity for intimacy with God in the next world. One of the great blessings of the Baptism of the Holy Spirit is that it opens the soul to a greater awareness and response to the presence of God—either in audible praise or in silent and rapt adoration. Vance Havner once wrote "God does not have His favorites, but He does have His intimates." In the area of communion and worship, the church at large very badly needs to grow.

My Growth in Relation to People

One way in which we must be conformed to the likeness of

Jesus is in the area of our relations to people. Jesus said He came not to be ministered unto, but to minister. All are required to be His witnesses and to preach the gospel to every creature. It has to begin there. If souls are not born into the family of God, there will be none to begin the process of growth. If you want to know which comes first, the chicken or the egg, the answer in this case is, of course, the egg.

Not only is God calling for soul-winners, but also for faithful laborers in His kingdom. Most churches suffer for lack of enough dedicated workers, so the burden for the many services of church and Sunday school fall upon the shoulders of the already overladen few. (To him that hath shall more be given.) But the serious Christian who is looking for rewards in heaven will follow the example of Jesus in His role as servant.

My Growth in Relation to Satan

Here we must tread gingerly. We are told to "resist the devil and he will flee from you" (James 4:7). We are also given authority over him: "Behold I give unto you power . . . over all the power of the enemy" (Luke 10:19). In Revelation we are told that "they overcame him (Satan) by the blood of the Lamb and by the word of their testimony" (12:11). And in Ephesians we read about spiritual warfare against principalities and powers and wicked spirits in high places (6:11-13).

Much has been written on the subject of how to handle Satan, some of which is controversial. Since we are talking about growth from spiritual infancy into full maturity, it would be well to honestly appraise our spiritual age before we attempt to engage in major conflicts with Satan. Many older Christians and also those young in the Lord do successfully resist the devil and find him to flee. This is as it should be.

Attempts at exorcism and major deliverance is something else. Until one has achieved greater maturity or giftedness, it is my opinion that it would be best to resist the devil in simpler ways. We can leave the big jobs to those especially called and qualified persons who have proved that they can handle them. In this area the church desperately needs those who can be entrusted with this very needful ministry.

Growth in Relation to Ourselves, the Inner Man

This is another facet of Christian growth which receives altogether too little emphasis. Yet, when we consider how much of the New Testament is devoted to commands and instructions on the development of Christian virtues and the weeding out of the vices of the self-life, we must surely understand that God attaches far more importance to what we *are* than to what we *do*.

Early in His call to His disciples, Jesus laid down an important principle: ". . . If any man will come after me, let him deny himself and take up his cross and follow me" (Matt. 16:24). When Jesus returned to Nazareth after the episode in the temple, when He was twelve, He was subject to Joseph and Mary (Luke 2:51). His self-humbling began long before He ever went to the cross.

The most difficult place to live the abundant and victorious Christian life is in the home. One sad fact concerning some public religious figures is that not all of them are in private what they appear to be in public. Although a very few of them might be fakes and hypocrites, most are not. They are simply human beings who "have this treasure in earthen vessels" (2 Cor. 4:7), and who have not followed the example of the Apostle Paul when he said, "I keep under my body, and bring it into subjection: lest . . . when I have preached to others, I myself should be a castaway" (1 Cor. 9:27).

Portraying a false image, whether consciously or unconsciously, does not apply to public figures only. Consider ourselves. How much difference is there between the image we project to the people we meet in church and the one we reveal to our husbands, wives, children and in-laws?

A missionary told me that one of the great problems on the mission field is that the missionaries don't get along with each other. The real test of a man's spiritual size is not how he presents or represents Christ in public, but how he does it in his own home and among his day-to-day associates. It is this that separates the men from the boys in spiritual stature.

However, when God sets before us this high standard—that we become like His Son—He does not mean to discourage but to challenge us. He does not expect the impossible and knows that the majority of His sons will become conformed only in varying degrees.

It is true that often new Christians become so enamored of God and so wholly dedicated to Him, that they make more progress in a few years than some old-timers do in a lifetime. But normally, it requires time for an apple to grow from blossom to small green sphere, to a ripe, sweet Jonathan.

God takes everything into consideration: the nation in which we were born, the times, the political, economic, cultural environment and the centuries of heredity which make up the totality of what we are by nature.

In thus considering our capacity, He does not expect the same performance of a one-talent person that He does of a five-talent one. What He does look for is faithfulness in reaching our individual potential. He commended the two-talent man as much as He commended the five-talent one. But He severely reprimanded the slothful servant.

Jesus grew in four areas: in His relation to God, to man, to Satan, and to himself. We can also grow in the same areas, into the image and likeness of God—a mature saint. It is not likely, however, that many of us will become as perfect a man as He was, developed in every part of His being. Maybe the Lord doesn't even expect that of us. Some of us are active by nature, others contemplative. Some do God's footwork, others do the kneework. So thank God for both, they are equally indispensable.

I am sure God wants well-balanced Christians, but if we should have bulges in some places and depressions in others, let us at least bulge as hard as we can. It is the slothful, indifferent Christians that God can hardly stand. Remember the rhyme—

> You can't go to heaven in a rockin' chair;
> The Lord don't have any lazy folks there.

Come to think of it, there probably will be a lot of lazy folks up there, but they will be in the category which Hal Lindsey called "the hippies of heaven."

Rewards are given to those who *earn* them by diligence: ". . . he is a rewarder of them that diligently seek him" (Heb. 11:6). The Apostle Paul tells us that prizes are given to those who win them by strenuous effort and dedication.

Do you remember how, on a racing-track, every competitor runs, but only one wins the prize? Well, you ought to run with your minds fixed on winning the prize! Every competitor in athletic events goes into serious training. Athletes will take tremendous pains—for a fading crown of leaves. But our contest is for a crown that will never fade.

I run the race then with determination. I am no shadowboxer; I really fight! I am my body's sternest master, for fear that when I have preached to others I should myself be disqualified (1 Cor. 9:24-27, PHILLIPS).

162

CHAPTER 21

Growing Pains, Part Two

Means of Growth

The great heavenly parent who set the standard of what He expects, which is likeness to Christ, has provided many means to achieve this goal, "According as his divine power hath given unto us all things that pertain unto life and godliness . . ." (2 Pet. 1:3).

1. The Bible
2. Prayer
3. The Holy Spirit
4. Apostles, prophets, evangelists, pastors, teachers to edify the body of Christ (Eph. 4:11-12)
5. Our brethren in Christ to help "Bear ye one another's burdens" (Gal. 6:2)
6. Music, "speaking to yourselves in psalms and hymns and spiritual songs" (Eph. 5:19)
7. Christian TV, radio, cassette tapes
8. Christian magazines, papers and books

The implementing of all these means should be enough to furnish us all with shining wings and glittering halos!

Some churches do not provide teaching of sufficient depth

163

to aid the serious Christian; hence an important way for him to receive help is from books devoted to advancing the deeper Christian life. I endorse this method because it was through *Waiting on God* by Andrew Murray and *A Short and Easy Method of Prayer*, by Madam Guyon (the latter out of print), that I learned the priceless art of silent contemplation and worship. It resulted in a profound and lasting spiritual change.

Christian bookstores or catalogs list many excellent books on subjects such as prayer, praise, humility, the Holy Spirit, and scripture study. Among the scores of "growth authors" are Hannah Whitall Smith, Andrew Murray, Donald Gee, Catherine Marshall, Merlin Carothers, Dr. Robert Frost, and Watchman Nee.

Regarding the reading of spiritual books, a caution is necessary. "Knowledge puffeth up, but charity edifieth" (1 Cor. 8:1). We can be deceived into thinking that *knowing* about deeper truths can be equated with *practicing* them. Changes come only by implementing this knowledge.

How-to Methods

How to attain to spiritual maturity is a big subject, defined in many ways by various theologians and denominations. All kinds of "keys" and "secrets" are offered: The right kind of thinking, giving, vocal confession of scripture, total surrender, acceptance, praise, love.

To the dedicated seeker after Christ-likeness, the method to use may present a problem. Actually, we cannot be arbitrary about methods. What helps one person might not help the other. God leads each person along an individual path. Even the very means that produced growth five or two years ago may do nothing later. As we grow, however slowly, we will require different methods and different kinds of spiritual food.

God Our Guide

It is good to remember that just as parents assume the responsiblility for the development of their children, so does our heavenly Father. He is the author and finisher of our faith. He will do all in His power to bring us into the depths of himself and will take us as far as we want to go.

He will encourage, plead with and even discipline His sons. However, one thing God will not do is impose His will on ours. If we rebel or only partially cooperate, our progress will be impeded. Our response to our Father's oversight of our growth will determine the rate and degree of our development.

Having in mind His eternal purpose, God apportions to each of us the right amounts of sunshine and shadow, joy and sorrow, trial and triumph.

That great exponent of the deeper Christian life, A.B. Simpson wrote: "Every moment the great refiner is waiting to add some new touch to your beauty and strength and to fit you for a higher place in His eternal life" ("Try Me," Randleman, North Carolina: Pilgrim Tract Society).

When Bunyan was in heaven, he talked to someone there who was able to look at his life from the perspective of the other side.

"I have seen toward myself not only the necessity and justice but even the mercifulness of the very afflictions that I once (when upon the earth) imputed to His severity. And I am now fully convinced no stroke I met with in the world below (and I met with many as well as great afflictions) either came sooner or fell heavier or stood longer than was needful. And I am sure my hopes were never disappointed but to secure my title to better things than what I had hopes for" (*Visions*, p. 31).

If we will have the right attitude and cooperate with His

165

Spirit, God will be able to bring us into the greatest spiritual growth in our inner lives of which we are capable in each of the four areas: Our relations to God, to man, to Satan, and to ourselves.

Price of the Prize

Salvation is received, rewards are earned and prizes are won.

One day James and John, the sons of Zebedee, said to Jesus, "Grant unto us that we might sit, one on thy right hand, and the other on thy left hand, in thy glory" (Mark 10:37). To which Jesus replied, ". . . can ye drink of the cup that I drink of?" (v. 38). When they said they could, Jesus told them that this privilege of high positions "shall be given to them for whom it is prepared of my Father" (Matt. 20:23).

After this incident, the first clue Jesus gave as to the nature of His cup was to inform them that heavenly standards for greatness were different than earthly ones. For ". . . whosoever will be great among you, shall be your minister: And whosoever of you will be the chiefest, shall be servant of all" (Mark 10:43-44).

Many Christians glibly acknowledge with the sons of Zebedee "Yes, I agree we must suffer in order to reign with Him" (2 Tim. 2:12, my paraphrase). But to pay the price is another thing.

Too many Christians feel it is not necessary to "go overboard" in spiritual matters. They attend church, read the Bible some, pay tithes, witness now and then, are honest in business. In short, they are nice, comfortable Christians. But unless they eventually do better than that, they will never exchange their bottles of milk for crowns.

I am acquainted with a devout woman whose husband was a habitual drunkard, for whom she prayed many years. For their childrens' sake and for his own soul's sake, she did not yield to her frequent temptations to divorce him. Hundreds of times she forgave her husband, fought against bitterness, exercised longsuffering. Because of this, she said she can now forgive anyone of anything and be patient under any circumstance.

The Lord took her a step further. She had sometimes confided her troubles to friends, but the Lord made her know she was to seek Him alone for sympathy and comfort. When she did so, she learned to lean on the bosom of Jesus.

This is the stuff saints are made of. And there are many of them, some hidden and others well known. That rare saint, Sundar Singh of India, whose writings I have often quoted, paid dearly for his crown. Driven from home when he became a Christian Sadhu or "holy man," he traveled on foot through India and Tibet, having no certain dwelling place, carrying only a Bible and necessities. He spent much time alone with God in caves and in other solitary places. No wonder God was able to give him spiritual experiences and visions of the next world, granted to only a few!

John Bunyan, whose writings I also quote, spent twelve years in prison for preaching without a license. Three years after his release, he was again imprisoned for a short period. His prison cell became the "office" in which he wrote many books.

In order that "they might obtain a better resurrection" some of the Christians mentioned in Hebrews 11 also paid a great price. "They were stoned, they were sawn asunder, were tempted, were slain with the sword: they wandered about in sheepskins and goatskins; being destitute, afflicted, tormented. . ." (v. 37; see also 35-40).

St. Paul also suffered greatly. And yet he said he counted "all things but loss for the excellency of the knowledge of Christ Jesus my Lord; for whom I have suffered the loss of all things, and do count them but dung, that I may win

Christ" (Phil. 3:8). He did all this in order that he would "finally be all that Christ saved me for and wants me to be" (Phil. 3:12, TLB).

Christians who catch the same vision will say ". . . the sufferings of this present time are not worthy to be compared with the glory which shall be revealed in us" (Rom. 8:18). And that therefore, as Paul said, so they also say "I strain to reach the end of the race and receive the prize for which God is calling us up to heaven. . ." (Phil. 3:14, TLB).

The Joy Set Before Us

Despite their sufferings, dedicated, prayerful and sacrificial Christians do not consider such a life a hardship, for they have found that ". . . the path of the just is as the shining light, that shineth more and more unto the perfect day" (Prov. 4:18). Solomon wrote that. Paul, amid his many afflictions, often spoke of his great joy in the Lord. Jesus endured the cross, despising the shame because of the joy that was set before Him. To Him, the doing of God's will was a source of joy. "I delight to do thy will, O my God: yea, thy law is within my heart" (Ps. 40:8). In fact, Jesus was the happiest man on earth, for it is said of Him that "You love right and hate wrong; so God, even your God, has poured out more gladness upon you than on anyone else" (Heb. 1:9, TLB).

The rewards of those who pay the price for growing into conformity to the likeness of Christ are not all future. For even now on earth they enjoy the superlative blessings of close fellowship with God. Nevertheless, many rewards await them in the world to come. Call it "pie in the sky" if you will, but some Christians will be enjoying that pie for a long, long time.

SECTION THREE

Heaven

By faith Moses, when he was come to years, refused to be called the son of Pharaoh's daughter; Choosing rather to suffer affliction with the people of God, than to enjoy the pleasures of sin for a season; Esteeming the reproach of Christ greater riches than the treasures in Egypt: for he had respect unto the recompense of the reward. By faith he forsook Egypt, not fearing the wrath of the king: for he endured as *seeing him who is invisible.*

Hebrews 11:24-27, italics mine

CHAPTER 22

Differences in Degrees of Glory and Capacities

It's a clear summer night. You are relaxing on a lawn chair in your backyard, head tilted, looking up at the stars. From hazy recollections of high school astronomy you tell yourself that some of the lights in the immensity above you are fixed stars, others are planets. As your gaze roams over the sky, you recall a few other facts.

In our solar system are nine planets, not one identical to the other. Venus is the bright one, called the evening star; Saturn has the rings; Mars is mysteriously marked; Jupiter is so big it could hold all the planets, with room for more; and little Pluto is so small that it was discovered by merest chance.

Vaguely you understand that the stars are also dissimilar. You notice that some are brighter and more easily seen than others. Suppose you visit your planetarium next weekend. You would then learn that stars do indeed vary, from the brilliant ones called "giants," which are up to one hundred times larger than our sun (also a star), down to several varieties of "white dwarfs," much smaller than our sun. Combinations range from twins, triplets, small groups like the Seven Sisters, up to huge masses, called globular clusters.

So the next time you sit in your backyard looking up at the star-studded dome, you will be aware that the heavenly bodies differ in chemical composition, degrees of heat or cold, distance, size and brightness.

Strangely, we find inequalities mentioned in 1 Corinthians 15, the resurrection chapter. "There is one glory of the sun, and another glory of the moon, and another glory of the stars; for one star differeth from another star in glory" (v. 41). However, the apostle who wrote these words was not giving a lesson in astronomy, for he adds, "So also is the resurrection of the dead" (v. 42).

Centuries later, John Bunyan was informed by his angelic escort that the inhabitants of heaven are not the same in degrees of glory (*Visions*, p. 29). And in our times, Gordon Lindsay wrote that in heaven "There will be great differences in rank and position of the saved in the next age" (*Paradise*, p. 28).

Most Christians are familiar with this passage in the Book of Daniel: "And they that be wise [teachers] shall shine as the brightness of the firmament; and they that turn many to righteousness as the stars forever and ever" (12:3). Some of these believers have assumed that those who qualify as "wise teachers" and as soul winners, will all shine with equal intensity. According to the Apostle Paul (1 Cor. 15:41-42), this is not necessarily so.

Singh appears to refer to 1 Corinthians 15 when he shares with us something he learned while in heaven: "The *degrees* of goodness reached by the soul of a righteous man is known by the [degree] of brightness that radiates from his whole appearance. For character and nature show themselves in the form of various glowing rainbow-like colors of great glory" (*Visions*, p. 29). Interestingly, when light passes through a prism, it is seen in the colors of the rainbow.

The figure of light is very frequently used in the New Testament.

For God, who commanded the light to shine out of darkness, hath shined in our hearts, to give the light of the knowledge of the glory of God in the face of Jesus Christ. (2 Cor. 4:6)

. . . God is light and in him is no darkness at all (1 John 1:5). Jesus said He was the light of the world. All of heaven is filled with light. In fact, we read that ". . . the city had no need of the sun, neither of the moon, to shine in it; for the glory of God did lighten it, and the Lamb is the light thereof" (Rev. 21:23).

When Jesus was on the Mount of Transfiguration, His inner light shone forth through his physical being, to become visible to the apostles. And since Jesus lives within each believer, could it not be that the measure of light which each Christian possesses corresponds to the degree to which Christ has been "formed" in him (Gal. 4:19)?

Differences in spiritual appearance among those in heaven should not surprise us. For on earth we observe great variety in degrees of spirituality among denominations, churches and individual Christians. Distinctions among Christians in your own church, for instance, are quite apparent. Some are careless, some are dedicated, and others are in between. In various ways, these differences are usually, but not always, seen in the countenance. The scripture says "They looked unto him, and were lightened [radiant]: and their faces were not ashamed" (Ps. 34:5).

A certain something on the faces of some Christians immediately identifies them as being followers of Christ. I heard of a commercial photographer who photographed a group of Sunday school teachers. He commented later that the faces of those people were noticeably different than the usual.

173

Yet, though Christians in general do have that mark of "family" relationship, certain ones are especially radiant with the glory and presence of God. Most of the time, however, what we really are within is seen and known by God alone. In heaven it will be manifest to all because what we are within will shine forth for all to see.

As the heavenly bodies vary in glory, so, the apostle wrote, will the souls in heaven—in brightness, in positions of service, in rewards and in groupings or associations among themselves.

Differences in Capacities

There is still another kind of distinction and it is by far the most important. It is not the diversities between saint and saint. It will be the differences in relationships between each saint and the Lord himself!

As a matter of fact, the reason why saints do differ among themselves is because their relationships to God differ. When Bunyan was in heaven he was informed, "The happiness and glory which all the blessed here enjoy is the result of their communion with and love to the ever blessed God, whose beautiful vision is the eternal spring from whence it flows. The more we see, the more we love; and love assimilates our souls into the nature of the blessed object of it, and thence results our glory.

"This makes a difference in the degrees of glory. Nor is there any murmuring in one to see another's glory much greater than his own. The ever blessed God is an unbounded ocean of light and life and joy and happiness, still filling every vessel that is put therein, till it can hold no more. And though the vessels are of several sizes, while each is filled there is none that can complain.

"My answer therefore to your question is that those who have the most enlarged faculties do love God most and are

174

thereby assimilated most into His likeness, which is the highest glory heaven can give" (*Visions*, pp. 28-29).

Dr. Robert Frost said something similar: "A friend of mine had a vision of heaven. Among other things, he saw people as glasses, all filled to overflowing, but of different capacities" (*Set My Spirit Free*, p. 192).

No matter how much God desires to impart himself to any one of his children, He can only do so to the limit of the capacity of that individual.

Among Christians, capacities vary in great degrees. The newly converted person, a spiritual babe, could be compared to a very small vessel. An aged saint, if he had been growing during his many years, should be mature in spirit with much larger capacity.

During one of his visits to heaven, Singh learned "In this world of spirits the spiritual progress of anyone governs the degree to which he is able to know and feel God. Christ reveals His glorious form to each one according to his spiritual enlightenment and capacity. If Christ were to appear in the same glorious light to the dwellers of . . . lower spheres of the spiritual world, as He appears to those in the higher plains, then they would not be able to bear it. So He tempers the glory of His manifestation to the state of progress and to the capacity of each individual" (*Visions*, pp. 30-31).

This illuminates the scripture in Revelation 3:21 in which the overcomer is promised that he can sit with Christ on His throne. It is evident that those able for such a position of closeness to God in His great glory would be the ones whose capacities had become enlarged by attaining to the greatest degrees of likeness to Christ.

There will always be differences among Christians. At one time Paul said to the Corinthians that he could speak to them only as to unspiritual, worldly people and as to babes in

Christ (1 Cor. 3:1, TAB). But to the Ephesians he wrote about God's desire that they grow up to the fullness of the stature of Christ. To the Ephesians also he wrote his tremendous prayer that they might be filled with all the fullness of God.

It is doubtful whether there have been or will be many who measure up to being "filled with all the fullness of God." But every Christian can grow up to the fullest of his own potential. We need not be discouraged if we feel that at present our capacity is small. As we diligently seek and serve the Lord, He can and will increase that capacity.

At one time in my Christian experience I feared that I had reached the limit of my capacity for further growth. I had gone through "a great and terrible wilderness" in which I had prayed for ten agonizing years for various spiritual victories. After they came, I was so happy in Christ that for years I seemed to coast along under a cloud of glory.

When I finally realized what was happening to me, I was deeply distressed and prayed that I might continue to grow. God answered that prayer. It seems that we need to be constantly prodded into seeking God by frequent trials and tribulations!

Thus we rejoice in the Lord, for He will work out all for our eternal good, as Matilda Nordtveldt wrote, "Who knows the position in eternity for which God is preparing us? Will we rebel against the painful training He is subjecting us to now, or will we use every adversity?" (*Live*, Gospel Publishing House, Springfield, Missouri).

We have no time to waste in feeling sorry for ourselves. There are prizes to be won, rewards to be earned, the eternal purpose of God to fulfill.

The only opportunity we have in which to prepare for the life which is to come is the brief span of our sojourn on this earth. In God's school there will be no making up of lessons in the next world.

C.S. Lovett in his book *Jesus Is Coming, Get Ready Christian*, said, "Only on earth do we find the conditions for bringing people to maturity. Only on earth can the image of God be developed into the likeness of God. The conditions necessary for changing people are not found in heaven. . . . It is on earth a man becomes a forgiving person. How does it come about? He has to be hurt by someone before he can forgive. Will there be any hurt in heaven? No. Then one cannot learn forgiveness there. How does a man develop patience? By encountering anxieties and frustrations, learning to absorb them in stride. Are they found in heaven? No.

"And how does a man become longsuffering? He has to suffer a long time. But we read there is no suffering in heaven. Therefore that trait too is developed on earth. So it is with every personality feature. Each is developed on earth where alone the conditions for change exist. There is no way for a man to mature in heaven; the necessary stresses are not found there.

"We have but this one life in which to change into the likeness of the Lord. Our personalities are formed as we react to His testings and trials of this life. What we finally become is up to us. We can be as sweet or sour as we like. We can let the blows of life shape us, or we can respond with hardness. We can remain the same person day in and day out, or we can let the circumstances of life change us every day" (Baldwin Park, California: Personal Christianity, pp. 50-51).

"Therefore we do not become discouraged. . . . Though our outer man is (progressively) decaying and wasting away, yet our inner self is being (progressively) renewed day after day. For our light, momentary affliction . . . is ever more and more abundantly preparing . . . and achieving for us an everlasting weight of glory, beyond all measure, excessively surpassing all comparisons and all calculations, *a vast and transcendent glory and blessedness never to cease!*" (2 Cor. 14:16-17, TAB italics mine).

CHAPTER 23

And So Shall We Ever Be with the Lord

The Bliss of Heaven

The believer's first emotion when he arrives in heaven will be the consummation of all that constitutes perfect bliss, satisfaction and fulfillment. He will be thrilled to be at last in his permanent home, that beautiful place which God has prepared for those who love and serve him. He will rejoice because there will be for him no more struggle with sin, no more attacks by Satan, no more sickness, hunger, poverty, bereavement, disappointment, loneliness or frustration.

They shall hunger no more, neither thirst any more, neither shall the sun light on them, nor any heat. (Rev. 7:16)

And God shall wipe away all tears from their eyes, and there shall be no more death, neither sorrow, nor crying, neither shall there be any more pain: *for the former things are passed away.* (Rev. 21:4, italics mine; see also Rev. 7:17)

But far greater than his delight at being in heaven will be the Christian's joy because he is with his Lord, whom having not seen he had loved, but whom he now sees face to face!

Therefore are they before the throne of God, and serve

him day and night in his temple: and he that sitteth on the throne *shall dwell among them.* (Rev. 7:15)
And they shall see his face; and his name shall be in their foreheads. (Rev. 22:4, italics mine; see also Rev. 22:3)

Those who on earth had experienced foretastes of the glory of His presence will now know it in fullness: ". . . in thy presence is fullness of joy; at thy right hand there are pleasures forevermore" (Ps. 16:11).

During his visit to heaven, Bunyan was given the following information by one of its inhabitants, "Below, the saints enjoy God in a measure, but here we enjoy Him without measure. There, they have some sips of His goodness, but here we have large draughts thereof and swim in the boundless ocean of happiness" (*Visions,* pp. 23-24).

The happiness of heaven has been confirmed hundreds of times by the testimonies of those who saw into heaven at the moment of death. It is also verified by those who had visions or who were taken into heaven. Their universal experience was that of joy and love so vast that it was beyond their ability to describe it. However, God gave John Bunyan the gift of expressing, in some measure, what heaven is like.

". . . By His glorious presence He makes heaven what it is; there being rivers of pleasures perpetually springing from the divine presence and radiating cheerfulness, joy and splendor to all the blessed inhabitants of heaven. . ." (*Visions,* pp. 15-16).

At this juncture, some may say, "If everybody will be so completely happy in heaven, then what is the point of striving so hard for rewards, and why should I make sacrifices to be such a wholly dedicated Christian?"

Here are the reasons why:

All Christians will go to heaven, but they will be assigned to different locations or planes.

All will have "mansions," but they will not be the same.

All will serve, but some in higher positions.
All will be happy, but some will be happier.

It Is a Matter of Degree.

We will receive in heaven only the treasures which we
have "laid up," the rewards which we have earned, the
spiritual maturity to which we have attained, the capacities
which we have developed while we were on the earth. If a
Christian had been complacent and careless, devoting
himself chiefly to "the good life," getting by with the very
least he could be and do for God, that is all he will have in
heaven.

On the other hand, if a Christian has been willing to strive
for the very best, he will have God's best awaiting him in
heaven. We will even determine, to some extent, the very
quality of heaven. Not only will we be the losers and the
poorer for not being diligent in seeking the Lord to grow, but
heaven itself will be the loser and the poorer for not having
enough mature sons to do the ministry up there and to
fellowship with God in fullness.

In the first chapter of his second letter, the Apostle Peter
enumerates various virtues which a Christian should "give
all diligence" to develop. The words "giving all diligence" in
the King James Bible (2 Pet. 1:5) are translated as follows in
other versions: work hard (TLB); do your utmost (PHILLIPS);
try your hardest (NEB); make every effort (RSV); adding all
earnestness (WEYMOUTH).

To those who by doing this "make [their] calling and
election sure" (2 Pet. 1:10) a wonderful promise is given:
"And so a triumphant admission into the eternal Kingdom of
our Lord and Saviour Jesus Christ shall be accorded to you"
(2 Pet. 1:11, WEYMOUTH). The poet must have had
something like this in mind when he wrote "Ten Thousand
Times Ten Thousand."

Ten thousand times ten thousand
In sparkling raiment bright,
The armies of the ransomed saints.
Throng up the steeps of light.
'Tis finished! all is finished!
Their fight with death and sin.
Fling open wide the golden gates
And let the victors in.

What rush of alleluias
Fills all the earth and sky!
What ringing of a thousand harps
Bespeaks the triumph nigh.
O day for which creation
And all its tribes were made!
O joy for all its former woes
A thousandfold repaid!

Henry Alford, 1810-1871

God's desire and plan over each child of His is that he shall have this kind of abundant, triumphant entrance into the heavenly kingdom.

The Judgment Seat of Christ

Up until now, we have been talking about entering heaven by the usual means—death. A great multitude has already gone there by this route. However, a much smaller company, by comparison, will get to heaven another way—by returning with Christ at His second coming.

Some time after this last event, when all the saints will be gathered on the other side, two other important events will take place: The judgment of the wicked dead and the judgment of believers. The wicked dead, who had already been confined in a place of torment, will receive their final judgment for their evil deeds.

The next event is called "The Judgment Seat of Christ," and refers to believers only. "For we must all have our lives laid open before the tribunal of Christ [judgment seat of Christ, KJV], where each must receive what is due to him for his conduct in the body, good or bad" (2 Cor. 5:10, NEB).

This term, "The Judgment Seat of Christ," does not mean a place of punishment for sins. The Greek word is *bema*. It simply means a tribunal or place of award at athletic events. These were popular and understood by those living in New Testament days. On these occasions winners were presented with awards, usually a crown of leaves. These were always well deserved, for each athlete had endured a period of strenuous training and sacrifice.

Several scriptures indicate that the early Christians were well instructed about the time of judgment of believers. John the Apostle wrote to the saints of his day "Love will come to its perfection in us when we can face the day of Judgment without fear; because even in this world, we have become as He is" (1 John 4:17, JB).

The same thought is expressed by the apostle when he wrote to them regarding the second coming of Christ. "And now, little children, abide in him; that, when he shall appear, we may have confidence, and not be ashamed before him at his coming" (1 John 2:28). Other versions say, "not shrink away," or be "embarrassed."

The athlete who knows that he has followed the rules of his trainer, that he has disciplined himself and made serious efforts to excel, will face the day of his *bema* with joyous assurance and confidence.

To project our thoughts to the end of time, we can see all of God's "athletes" of whatever sort awaiting their awards. Imagine a multitude of the saints of all the ages of time, from Adam down to the last convert, assembled before the great Tribunal. One by one, each Christian stands before Christ, while His eyes pierce into the innermost being. "Neither is there any creature that is not manifest in his sight; but all things are naked and opened unto the eyes of him with whom we have to do" (Heb. 4:13).

It would be easy to imagine how some Christians will feel when they see others getting large rewards, while they get small ones, and know that is all they deserve. Others may receive none at all, being those who were "saved . . . so as by fire," and who will "suffer loss" (1 Cor. 3:15).

Some Christians will learn at this time that they will remain forever in a lower plane in heaven than God had planned and desired for them. Others will be dismayed to learn that they had qualified themselves only for lesser positions of service, while another group will become sadly aware that they had developed a very limited capacity for eternal fellowship with Christ.

Will these kinds of Christians be disappointed? Will they have regrets when they look back on their lives and see wasted opportunities, carelessness, indifference, sloth?

But you say, "Regrets in heaven? How can that be! I thought that in heaven there will be no sorrow."

I don't know how that will be. I can suggest that if there is a period of regret, that it will certainly not be permanent. The Book of Revelation says in two places "And God shall wipe away all tears from their eyes" (7:17; 21:4).

It could be that after the "moment of truth" (however long it would last, for we are now in eternity, not in time) that God would afterward "wipe away all tears" and enable us to adjust to our state and condition in heaven.

However that will be, we do know that Christians will finally be perfectly content in heaven because it would be impossible to be otherwise in the presence of God.

Heaven will be all you thought it would be and far, far more. For "eye hath not seen, nor ear heard," nor has heart imagined how wonderful it will be, even for those in the lowest planes (1 Cor. 2:9).

But it will be even more glorious for the believers whose dedicated Christian living has won for them "mansions" in higher levels of heaven, who will shine with greater degrees of glory, and whose maturity has fitted them for deeper fellowship with God.

Nevertheless, God so greatly loves His children, whatever their spiritual state, that He will be spending all of eternity making them happy and fulfilled. "That in the ages to come he might show the exceeding riches of his grace in his kindness toward us through Christ Jesus" (Eph. 2:7).

You may be surprised and disappointed at the way this book is ending. If you are, perhaps it's the best thing that could happen to you. Wouldn't it be far better to have a "rude awakening" while you still have a chance to make changes than to have it happen on the day of judgment?

As long as we are still in the body, we have time to ". . . lay aside every weight, and the sin which doth so easily beset us, and . . . run with patience the race that is set before us," (Heb. 12:1).

If it will cost something, then let us by all means pay the price. The Apostle Paul called all that he sacrificed "rubbish."

But those things I used to consider gain I have now reappraised as loss in the light of Christ. I have come to rate all as loss in the light of the surpassing knowledge of my Lord Jesus Christ. For His sake I have forfeited everything; I have accounted all else rubbish so that Christ may be my wealth. . . . (Phil. 3:7-8; NAB)

In his letter to the Romans the apostle said, "For I reckon that the sufferings of this present time are not worthy to be compared with the glory which shall be revealed in us" (Rom. 8:18).

If we "press toward the mark for the prize of the high calling of God in Christ Jesus" (Phil. 3:14), as Paul did, we will be assuring ourselves of our fullest happiness in heaven. But much more important than that, we will be pleasing God by fulfilling His eternal purpose and plan over us.

We must hurry, though, for as Amy Carmichael said, "We have all eternity to celebrate the victories, but only a few hours before sunset to win them" (*Live*).

Briefly Biographical

Sadhu Sundar Singh

Sundar Singh, author of *Visions of Sadhu Sundar Singh of India*, was born into a wealthy and intellectual Sikh family in India in 1889. He was converted in his youth. Cast out by his father, Sundar became a Christian Sadhu or holy man, traveling and preaching in India and Tibet. In later years he ministered to thousands in America, England, and other countries. Between preaching missions he returned to solitude, simplicity and prayer. He lived so close to God that even today his name is respected by Christians in India and elsewhere.

Regarding his visions, he wrote "At Kotgarh, fourteen years ago, while I was praying, my eyes were opened to the Heavenly Vision. So vividly did I see it all that I thought I must have died and that my soul had passed into the glory of heaven. Throughout the intervening years these visions have continued to enrich my life.

"I cannot call them up at will. Usually when I am praying or meditating—sometimes as often as eight or ten times in a month—my spiritual eyes are opened to see within the heavens. For an hour or two I walk in the glory of the heavenly sphere with Christ Jesus and hold converse with angels and spirits. Their answers to my questions have provided much of the material that has already been published in my books. The unutterable ecstasy of that spiritual communion makes me long for the time when I shall permanently enter the bliss and fellowship of the redeemed" (p. 5).

Marietta Davis

In the summer of 1848, when Marietta Davis was twenty-five-years old, she became ill and lay in a coma for nine days. Later, she said she had been in a trance and in heaven during this time. She lived for seven more months and died at the exact day and hour which she had predicted.

Her pastor, Mr. J.L. Scott, recorded her vision, using her own style of narrative. The book *Scenes Beyond the Grave* was widely read and accepted by the conservative denominations of her day. Up to the present, it has passed through twenty-nine editions and is still being read.

John Bunyan

Bunyan lived in England in the seventeenth century. His sins caused him such misery that he entered a woods, planning to commit suicide, when a voice from heaven stopped him. Deeply moved, he fell on his knees and gave himself fully to God. While thanking the Lord, he was surrounded by light and an angel took him into heaven. When he returned home, he took [his] pen and ink and wrote down what [he] had heard and seen, declaring the whole vision from first to last (p. 63), *Visions of Heaven and Hell.*

He became a Nonconformist preacher and, for preaching without a license, was imprisoned for twelve years, during which time he read his Bible, prayed, and wrote. After his release, he was again imprisoned, this time for a shorter period. He then wrote *Pilgrim's Progress*, for which he is best known.

Daisy Dryden

Daisy was the daughter of a Methodist minister. A few days before her death in 1864 at the age of ten, she informed her father that she had seen Jesus and He told her she was going to heaven, to Him.

She lingered for three days, during which time she saw into heaven and frequently communicated with her deceased brother, Allie. She herself said the reason she could do this was because she had "dying eyes."

Her mother, who wrote *Visions of Heaven*, says there were various evidences of her being perfectly rational up to the last and "therefore fully credible in all her statements." Writing an introduction to the book, F. L. Higgins said, "What was remarkable in Daisy's case of opened vision was its unusual length and the clearness of her revelations . . ." (p. 6).

Elizabeth Bossert

After a period of illness, on June 8, 1948, Elizabeth

Bossert knew she was dying. She said goodbye to her family and as she closed her eyes, felt herself going up into the next world. She later recorded her experiences, after she revived, in *My Visit to Heaven*.

Bibliography

Bramwell Booth. *Visions*. New York: The Salvation Army, 1906.

Elizabeth Bossert. *My Visit To Heaven*. Jacksonville, Florida: Higley, 1968.

John Bunyan. *Visions of Heaven and Hell*. Swengel, Pennsylvania: Reiner, 1966.

Joseph Miles Chamberlin and Thomas D. Nicolson. *Planets, Stars and Space*. Manketo, Minnesota, n.d.

Winston Churchill. *The Hinge of Fate: The Second World War*, vol. 4. Boston: Houghton, Mifflin, 1950.

S.H. Dryden. *Visions of Heaven*. Minnesota: Osterhus, 1946.

Robert C. Frost. *Set My Spirit Free*. Plainfield, New Jersey: Logos International, 1973.

Billy Graham. *Angels, God's Secret Agents*. New York: Doubleday, 1975.

Myrna Grant. *Vanya*. Carol Stream, Illinois: Creation House, 1974.

Oliver B. Greene. *Heaven*. Greenville, South Carolina: The Gospel Hour, n.d.

Gordon Lindsay. *Paradise, Abode of the Righteous Dead*. Dallas, Texas: The Voice of Healing, 1967.

Gordon Lindsay, compiler. *True Visions of the Unseen World*. Dallas Texas: The Voice of Healing, n.d.

Hal Lindsey. *There's A New World Coming*. Santa Ana, Vision House, 1973.

C.S. Lovett. *Jesus Is Coming, Get Ready Christian*. Baldwin Park, California: Personal Christianity, 1969.

Thoburn C. Lyon. *Witness in the Sky*. Chicago: Moody Press, 1961.

Catherine Marshall. *To Live Again*. New Jersey: Fleming H. Revell, 1957.

Raymond A. Moody. *Life after Life*. Atlanta: Mocking Bird Books, 1975.

Arthur D. Morse. *While Six Million Died*. New York: Random House, 1967.

Norman Vincent Peale. *The Power of Positive Thinking*. New Jersey: Prentice Hall, 1952.

Karl Sabiers. *Where Are the Dead?* Los Angeles: Christian Pocket Books, 1959.

J.L. Scott, *Scenes Beyond the Grave*. Dallas: The Voice of Healing, n.d.

Sundar Singh. *The Visions of Sadhu Sundar Singh of India*, Minneapolis: Osterhus, n.d.

Anne Terry White. *All About the Stars*. New York: Random House, 1954.

M. Woodworth-Etter. *Signs and Wonders*. Indianapolis: Lakeview Temple, n.d.

Pamphlets, Articles and Tracts

Marvin S. Ford. "Thirty Minutes in Heaven," *Full Gospel Business Men's Voice* 24 (1976):9.

Carol Hooley. *Caught Up To Heaven*. Denver: Liberty Publications, n.d.

"Life after Death," *Guideposts*. Carmel, New York, n.d.

Betty Malz. *Twenty-four Hours*. Pasadena, Texas: by author, n.d.

Judson B. Palmer. *The Child of God between Death and Resurrection*. Minneapolis: Osterhus, n.d.

The Woman Who Saw Heaven. Randleman, North Carolina: Pilgrim Tract Society, n.d.